Life in the Spirit

Life in the Spirit

True Stories of Blessings, Favor, and Intervention

William Porter

TATE PUBLISHING
AND ENTERPRISES, LLC

Published by Tate Publishing & Enterprises, LLC
127 E. Trade Center Terrace | Mustang, Oklahoma 73064 USA
1.888.361.9473 | www.tatepublishing.com

Tate Publishing is committed to excellence in the publishing industry. The company reflects the philosophy established by the founders, based on Psalm 68:11,
"The Lord gave the word and great was the company of those who published it."

Cover design by Junriel Boquecosa
Interior design by Jake Muelle

Published in the United States of America

ISBN: 978-1-68028-370-9
1. Religion / Christian Life / Inspirational
2. Religion / Christianity / Holy Spirit
15.05.11
Available in Spanish

This book is dedicated to my parents. To my mother, Minnie (Minnetta), who loved the Lord more than anyone I know and to my father, Porter, who introduced me to basic Bible scriptures at an early age.

Acknowledgments

This work would not have been completed without the blessings, favor, and intervention of God through the Holy Spirit in various circumstances of the author's life. There are several individuals who were instrumental in the completion of this work. Special thanks to my wife, Yvonne, for her understanding and support in the time spent in preparing this document. Appreciation is also extended to my daughters, Panya and Pamela, who, knowingly or unknowingly, gave me a lot of material to work with in the creation of some of the stories. And then, there is James Earl, my brother, who gave me valuable input as to the protocol involved in the distribution of the final product. My other brother Alvin also supplied some of the photographs. Special thanks to Pastor Staccato Powell who constantly provided spiritual leadership and wrote the forward to the book. To the other persons who lent their support, in one way or the other, to the production of this work, I am eternally grateful.

Contents

Foreword

One of the many privileges of pastoring a flock of people is becoming familiar with the array of gifts sitting in a congregation. This is how I encountered William Porter. Initially, it was his late wife who chose to connect with the church where I served as pastor. Subsequently, William and their two daughters started frequenting the Sunday worship and Tuesday Bible study. William, a quiet, thoughtful, and reserved individual, one Sunday as the invitation to discipleship and membership was being extended, popped up and, without hesitation, strolled down to the front of the church and connected to the Grace African Methodist Episcopal Zion Church in Raleigh, North Carolina.

It was then that I discovered this academic genius of multiple talents. Here is a glimpse of one such talent and gift. A thoughtful man who personifies the adage, "Still waters run deep," Porter has taken the time to compile various stories that reveal the hand of God in everyday situations. Often we only define the miraculous as being an extraordinary supernatural occurrence on a grand scale that defies logic. *Life in the Spirit* grants us insight into the not-so common-daily-move of God in mysterious ways His wonders to perform.

Whether it is having your car almost empty of fuel coming to rest in front of a gas pump prior to completely stopping in the middle of an a busy intersection or what appears to be a chance meeting of a future spouse at a street festival, Porter would contend it is all due to divine intervention. Often we fail to realize and overlook such enormous blessings and attribute it to luck.

Life at its best is lived in the Spirit. This compilation of stories has been chosen to demonstrate the timely nature of God's providence and perpetual presence. Being the benefactor of God's "blessings, favor, and intervention" is not confined to sacred settings and space. Many instances of the move of God on our behalf go unacknowledged because of our inability to connect the dots. Here, Porter, in an unadorned and straightforward fashion, illustrates God's constant care of His children.

I encourage the reader to add your own account of "favor, blessings, and intervention" to this collection of anecdotes depicting the pragmatic power of an awesome God. If ever one needs a poignant but simple reminder of God's promise of His perpetual presence, *Life in the Spirit* will provide it.

A debt of gratitude is owed to William Porter, Jr., Panya and Pam's dad and Yvonne's husband, for giving us this chronicle of living faith.

As a colleague shared with me recently, "Faith is acting on what we believe." *Life in the Spirit* demonstratively displays the biblical admonition "All things are possible if you only believe." May we chime in and declare, "Lord, we believe and help our unbelief."

—Dr. Staccato Powell

Introduction

Life in the Spirit is awareness that some events that happen in our lives are expressions of God's blessings, favor, and intervention. It is exciting when we recognize these events as such because then, we realize that God is a real, living entity and, therefore, is willing and able to help us when we are in need. Many churches have services during the week when believers assemble to give their testimonies of how God has blessed them. One of the biggest factors in increasing one's faith is to learn how God has been involved directly in the lives of people and how specific events have affected their faith. *Life in the Spirit* is a series of true stories about people in their everyday life and how they have been blessed and favored by God, or people who have been in situations where God, through the Holy Spirit, has intervened in very negative circumstances for their benefit. We all have had times when the things that have happened to us could not be explained rationally. It strengthens our faith knowing that God will help us in our time of need. This is especially so when we have evidence of being carried through some of life's trying circumstances. In reading the experiences of others who have been confronted with negative situations or circumstances, some may remember how God helped them in their own lives in their time of need.

This book is an accumulation of true stories that involve real events and circumstances that have happened to people in their everyday life. In order to document these situations, in some cases people were interviewed and they talked about their experiences involving what they felt were God's blessings, favor, or intervention in certain situations. In other instances, the stories are the product of the author's own experiences. The stories represent a variety of cultures where individuals function in their everyday life. Also, the stories are couched within the framework of the natural or cultural setting of the lead character. In order to get the entire benefit of what a story has to offer, it is necessary to read all of the story, which includes both the local setting and circumstances surrounding the lead character, as well as the blessing, favor, and/or intervention that person, as well as other characters in the story, may have experienced.

While the events and circumstances in this book are actual accounts of blessings, favor, and interventions from God as expressed by people in their personal lives, the names of the major characters in each story and the locations where events took place have been changed or altered out of respect for the privacy of those who shared their experiences. In addition, while the events in each story are true in regards to the documentation of people's accounts of what they felt were God's blessings some aspects of the story line may be altered to contribute to the general flow of the story.

It is also beneficial to realize that for some occasions in each story, biblical references are made that confirm a spiritual truth as seen by the author. Any reference reflects the culmination of years of Bible study, listening to sermons and teachings from the Scriptures, and enduring life's experiences. In this context, any believer can relate certain spiritual truths to their own lives. The Holy Spirit speaks to different people individually, so the reader may comprehend spiritual truths other than those that are expressed in this book. It is good that God speaks to us as individuals, and it is very exciting to realize that although we may have different opinions or interpretations on a given issue or Bible verse, we are unified, as the body of Christ, by the general truths expressed in the Scriptures.

Blessings, Favor, and Intervention

One of the great benefits of *Life in the Spirit* is God's blessings that come to us each and every day. These blessings may not be a dramatic manifestation of God's presence in our lives, but rather simply be the knowledge that God is our reality knowing that He is with us in everything we do, every place we go, and in every thought we have. While we make mistakes from time to time, He is aware of our every need. Feeling condemned or inadequate because we are doing less than what God expects us to do is not a viable option. It important however, to accept the major premise behind Christianity throughout the ages, and that is Jesus Christ came to this earth, over two thousand years ago, for a purpose, that purpose was to die for man's sins and to restore him to a right relationship with God. He continues to help us, as an intercessor to God the Father and through the Holy Spirit, to live the best possible life while we are alive on this earth (Psalm 37:4).

Life in the Spirit, then, is the Holy Spirit within us, who leads us to a sincere desire to do what God expects of us. God can then give us the strength to overcome whatever issues we may have. Then we can actively and confidently move toward that high standard God demands of us. The knowledge of this fact should give us great comfort in the face of our shortcomings and negative circumstances and is therefore one of God's greatest blessings.

> *Delight yourself also in the Lord, And He shall give you the desires of your heart.*
>
> —Psalm 37:4

PRESSURE AT THE PUMP

1

Nervous Drive

Be anxious for nothing, but in everything
by prayer and supplication, with thanksgiving,
let your requests be made known to God.

—Philippians 4:6

One of God's blessings happened to Paula, who loves God and loves her work. The day of the blessing started as any other day, with a bright sun rising in the eastern sky. Breakfast was prepared the night before. It was a delicious mixture of wheat bread and a combination of beef beacon and cheese with egg whites in between. Paula is very conscious of her diet so she always try to limit her time in the kitchen. So in the morning with her breakfast already prepared, she simply heated it up in the microwave oven, gobbled down the sandwich and away she went as she did every morning. She was off to work, concentrating on the busy schedule that she had before her.

Paula makes a real effort to be at work by eight and despite the traffic she usually makes it on time. Her busy day is abbreviated by a quick lunch; she usually goes to lunch alone, and there are several local eateries in the area around where she works. Occasionally, she may go with a coworker or have a lunch meeting at her job where she is still fulfilling work at lunchtime.

Being an architect she always is interested in how buildings are constructed. With her specialty area being HVAC she often examines interior designs especially and sometimes offers critiques of the heating and cooling systems ducts that can often be seen in local establishments.

Paula's work career is a product of her time in college where she participated in the band. While very active in extra curricula activities, she buckled down, so to speak, in her classes. They were demanding classes like geometry, physics and calculus. So Paula was well prepared for her newly acquired job after college, which consisted of a little engineering and a little architectural design where she obtained her degree. Therefore, she was quite proficient with inspections on buildings in other cities around the state. When she is working on a rather large project, often with co-workers, she loves the drawings that are required to complete the job. She had long since passed the engineering post undergraduate exam needed to be an apprentice where she can legally develop and put her stamp of approval on any drawings that she makes as part of the preparation for a construction project.

As Paula's workday comes to a close, she would soon begin the routine of activities away from the job. After a long day in the office, or perhaps out of town doing inspections, she was eager to return home to prepare dinner for herself. On a typical day as she would travel from work, there was the usual heavy traffic on her way home. The trip home was not very far, but the traffic was heavy that day, and she witnessed two accidents on the way. Finally, she would look forward to retire for an evening of personal activities.

After a long day in the office, she was eager to return home to prepare her evening meal. These moments in the afternoon are special, and being single, she looks forward to an evening of relaxation in solitude, meditation, and prayer. She also enjoys watching her favorite TV shows and is especially interested in the current events of the day. She may even start to prepare early for the vacation trip she is looking forward to. Time off from work is a very special period where she can just relax and review her commitments, both personal and professional, in her daily planner. She especially looks forward to taking her trip to the various islands of the Caribbean on her next vacation. Several years ago, she went to Cancun Mexico and enjoyed it a lot. She loved the pristine white-sand beaches with the crystalline waters. It is one of the most popular tourist destinations in the world, and Paula certainly can attest to why that's the case. What better way to spend your vacation than at one of the luxury hotel resorts in the area. Can you imagine spending a sultry night on your hotel patio gazing at the moonlit sky reflecting onto the shiny ocean waters below and sipping a margarita being serviced at your command? Well, enough of the dreaming. This time, she plans to visit to the Bahamas where, at a friend's urging, she will travel to the Exuma Islands. It brought memories of crystal-clear to sapphire-blue waters that can be seen in the lakes and ponds as well as off the beaches making up the many small islands of this tropical paradise. There are tours given where visitors can stroll along the many waterways in the area where nice private homes of famous movie stars and other celebrities can be seen along the coastline. But again, enough of the dreaming! She will need to make a decision on her next trip and go through the challenging process of selecting lodging accommodations, scheduling places to visit, and making airline reservations.

After an evening at home and a good night's rest, the next morning Paula's routine starts over again and the day promises to be a busy one, as usual. While blessings occur every day in our lives, usually we don't take the time to acknowledge how fortunate we are just to get out of bed, have reasonable health and strength, and knowing that we have a job to go to and a place called home to lay our heads. However, on this day Paula's blessing was truly one to remember.

Prior to coming home, she fights a busy rush hour traffic. Home was not very far, but traffic was heavy that day, and she witnessed two accidents on her way home. It could have lent itself to be a stressful situation, especially knowing that she needed to stop someplace and pump gas into her vehicle. Adding to her concern was that the gas needle was on empty. She had intended to fill her tank earlier but didn't get the chance. Besides, she has been in this position before and knew that she could drive for at least twenty additional miles with her gas needle in that position. But she still had five to ten miles before she could get to the nearest station. On top of that, the stop-and-go traffic had a tendency to drain what little gas she had. All of a sudden, she was anxious about making it to the next gas station.

Paula continues to drive, and with every passing minute she is concerned that she will run out of gas and become stranded on a busy street, still quite distant from a gas station. She decides to take the exit when she knows there is a station. She is hopeful but still unsure whether she will make it. Meanwhile, the dinner that was in her mind to prepare is now a distant thought, as she is more concerned about getting to the station and make it to the stoplight after making the exit. Thankfully, she finally arrives at the stoplight and the station she wishes to get to is in sight on the right! But while the station is in view, it is yet another half mile away, slightly downhill on the left side of the road.

She did make the right turn, but now, being almost out of gas, she had to depend on gravity to propel her car forward. So she used the brake pedal a lot as she moved on the gradual downhill. She had to be careful to press the accelerator pedal only slightly to conserve what little gas she had left in her car. "Thank the Lord for the downward grade in the road," Paula said to herself! And so, nature was Paula's biggest friend at that point. Though it was only a gradual decline of the road, it was enough of a downward grade to keep her car moving forward. She needed to use as little amount of gas as possible so that she could make it to that station!

As the force of gravity literally propelled her car forward, she eventually came near the intersection where the gas station was located. Almost there, she thought! Come on car, just a little further now, she uttered! Soon the car came almost to a stop on the street as it continued to drift, for only a few feet, to the front of the station. What made matters worse was there was traffic behind her, with some motorists growing impatient because of Paula's slow-moving vehicle being in front of them. In one instance, she heard someone honk their horn to get her moving faster. But she couldn't drive her car any faster. She was almost completely out of fuel! She could only hope that her car would not come to a complete stop in the middle of the street before getting to the front of the station and making the left turn to get her vehicle to an available pump.

At that point, Paula would need to make the left turn in front of oncoming traffic from the opposite direction to get to a pump at the station. If there were cars coming from the opposite direction, she obviously would need to stop and not make the turn. And she would rather not do that because the car might stall in the middle of the street just prior to making the turn!

Fortunately, there was no traffic coming from the opposite direction and she was able to let her car continue to roll and make the left turn into the station. With her car going so slow, would the steering wheel lock up? That thought crossed her mind briefly. Nonetheless, Paula made the left into the property of the station. Her vehicle then came to rest in front of one of the pumps. Her car would not go any further! But fortunately, she didn't have to go any further. She was at the pump! How convenient. Needless to say, Paula was blessed to have her car drift and stop where it did, in the exact place where it had to be given the circumstances. So Paula got out of her car, now confident that she could finally get some fuel so that she could continue her journey home.

But wait! Paula's problem was still not totally resolved. While her car did come to a stop in front of the gas pump, she found that the hose from the pump did not quite reach the gas cap to her car! Oh no! She had to tug a little on the flexible gas hose to get it to reach the entrance to the gas tank on her car! It turned out not to be just a little tug, she had to pull the hose with all her strength to stretch it so that the pump on the end of the hose would reach the gas cap on her car. At this point, she certainly didn't want to get any assistance, not after all the effort she had to put in getting her car to this position. With a grunt, she stretched the hose to the point where she was able to place the head of the fuel pump itself into the entrance to where the fuel would enter her vehicle. The hose turned out to be just the length she needed. She then proceeded to fill her car's gas tank with fuel.

A rather nervous drive ended successfully at a gas pump Paula desperately needed to get to in order to refuel. Afterward, she then continued home to a restful evening. That night, she certainly had a lot to be thankful for, as God's blessings, favor, and intervention was clearly with her that afternoon (Philippians 4:6).

> *Be anxious for nothing, but in everything by prayer and supplication, with thanksgiving, let your requests be made known to God.*
>
> —Philippians 4:6

THE WISDOM OF WAITING

2

Good Timin'

Trust in the Lord with all your heart,
And lean not on your own understanding.

—Proverbs 3:5

Have you noticed the one kid on your block that is a little bit different? John Rossart, a teacher at Highland Community College in Mansfield, New Hampshire was different and committed to his work. He had wit and a genuine love for his job, which was teaching English literature in the school's language department. John has taught at Highland for fifteen years and had established himself as a friendly fellow on the campus and did his job in a professional manner.

Highland is unique among institutions of higher learning in New Hampshire. While other colleges in the state focus on the arts, science and mathematics, and business, Highland's focus is on trade professions including drafting, home economics, and electronics. Many students have been attracted to these areas in the past because the curriculum here is not found at the most other institutions in the state. Nonetheless, enrollment at the relatively small school has been declining in recent years primarily because employers in these professions, formerly plentiful in the state, have since migrated to other areas of the country. This has had a negative effect on faculty and staff at the school, including John Rossart.

John has established himself at Highland, where he enjoys the small town feel of the local community. The area surrounding Mansfield, a small city of about fifty thousand in population, is surrounded by a largely rural environment. He loves hiking in the nearby White Mountains, which is the northern branch of the elongated Appalachian Mountain chain a few miles inland away from the eastern seaboard. One unusual hobby of his is hiking in the snow, and snow comes at a very early period in the autumn season of the year in this mountain region. In fact, locals start to plan for the long winter season even before the end of summer in late August and early September. You can see loggers out cutting down huge maple trees and reducing their huge trunks into fireplace lumber friendly logs. And yes, fireplaces are very common in New England. What better way to spend a cool autumn evening than by having a fireplace chat with your significant other, or the kids. Some of John's relatives often visit him, like at Thanksgiving and Christmas time.

John has a small grill and loves to cook on the weekends outside his condo patio just beyond the sliding glass door to his living room even when snow is on the ground several feet high. He loves to observe the snowy landscape, including the frosty trees and the pine needles that drift from the treetops of a portion of the coniferous forest to the snow-covered surface below. Occasionally, rabbits and perhaps a stray dog might be seen running around, apparently trying to seek shelter from the elements. It's not until later in

November when the temperature outside is so low that it's uncomfortable for John to be out grilling. Unless it's in the twenties and the wind is howling, he can somehow survive the elements quite well outside his sliding door on the patio. But even when he's not outside, the natural beauty of the snow environment can be appreciated from his living room. What better way to relax than grab some popcorn and a large mug of hot chocolate and just relax in front of the fireplace looking outside into the snowy abyss? Even at night, John likes to sit in his comfy chair near that sliding door with curtains drawn together with a dim lamp nearby. He enjoys this quiet time as he often reads his favorite novel while listening to the crackling sound of the logs emitting soft flames in the fireplace.

John's two nephews, Jason and Cephus, would sometimes come over, usually during the Thanksgiving and Christmas holidays. One time their parents brought them over the day after Thanksgiving. It was early in the afternoon. Once situated inside of John's condo, they began to relax and eventually grabbed some wieners John had in the refrigerator and placed them over the open flames! But not the open flames on John's grill outside on the patio. They would much rather be inside, preparing their food above the open flames of the huge fireplace in John's living room. The boys also enjoy one of John's favorite staples, baked beans that John usually heats in a skillet that hovers over the open flames of the fireplace. It has a smoked flavor that the kids really enjoy. During the evening, they all gather around the fireplace and listen to the radio because John has no television. As they listen to the howling wind outside, John would tell stories about his camping excursions in the nearby mountains. Once the kids get tired of hearing John's stories, they venture into a corner and play checkers. The kids would soon go to bed after that and have a good night's sleep. After a breakfast of sausage, eggs, and potatoes that John would prepare on his small gas stove in the kitchen along with a little orange juice, they are ready to go. They would then be picked up by their parents at seven. John would now be free to go on one of his camping excursions despite the brisk, cold, but fair conditions on this Saturday.

So while grilling at home is fine with John, his heart is in camping out in the mountains nearby and cooking food over an open campfire. So after school starts, which is in mid August, John has about a month before he can visit the various camping sites that are available for campers like himself, who enjoy the outdoors and especially the challenges the colder weather brings. He has all of the items he needs to survive and even enjoy the frigid but rewarding experience at his favorite site. This includes a snowpack, with all of the essential items necessary for a days' outing. Occasionally he would spend overnight with all the camping gear in place that he needs. And don't forget the extra pair of socks!

On one occasion, he probably overextended his stay at one campsite. He started on his way back home later than he should have after listening to a weather advisory warning campers of an approaching snowstorm. It was late afternoon, and John decided to have a quick meal before heading back. But the extra hour proved to be significant because as he drove the twenty miles from the campsite to his house, the rather calm but cloudy weather gave way to increased winds, and then snow flurries began. As the roads worsened from the accumulation of snow, he was fortunate in that the truck his was driving handled those conditions well. Nonetheless, the winds were howling to the point where it was difficult for John to keep his vehicle on the road. As he navigated through light traffic on the road at that time, he eventually made it back to his condo just before the heavy accumulation took place. It was good he came back when he did because as the evening grew on, blizzard conditions prevailed in the region for the remainder of that night.

So John really enjoyed living in the often-frigid environment of the New England mountains in late fall. Later during the winter, the snow accumulation is just too much, and the temperatures too low for any outside camping activity for John, so he spent most of his time inside, keeping as warm as possible. This type of environment is quite different from his home, Virginia, particularly in the coastal plain southeastern region of the state far from the mountains in the western portion of the state.

John attended undergraduate and graduate schools in Virginia and received the doctorate in his research area of language arts. He was employed on at least three other occasions in similar teaching positions, but those appointments were only temporary where he was released with only a short notice. So Highland turned out to be quite beneficial to him personally as well as professionally. You see, the school is located in a geographical area where he was very fond of as far as recreational activities were concerned. At Highland, would have the opportunity to enjoy the surrounding mountain environment. So thank goodness for Highland, where he was offered a long term contract over fifteen years ago. *Hopefully, disappointment won't rear its head again* as he anticipate being at the school for the remainder of his career.

One advantage that John had was that he is the only professor qualified to teach the English literature course at the school. So he felt really good about the chances of him finishing up his career at Highland. He has ten years left until retirement and looked forward to his remaining years at Highland. Plus there are a number of federally funded programs that he directs during the summer months in the training of middle and high school students in the subject area of English literature and it origins. The summer programs try to gear students to the much larger state institutions in the New England region, and John has a good track record in training kids in this area. So students are well prepared to tackle the heavy workload that is a part of most of the state's English literature curriculum.

Because of budgetary concerns, teachers have been terminated from Highland over the past two years. This comes as a blessing in disguise for many of them because there are other colleges in the state and across the nation where they can command a higher income. School administration had thought about budgetary cuts in a number of areas, including English literature. Some of John's friends in fact, have been laid off because of this reason. So it is a nervous time on campus because no one knows who will be next on the chopping block, so to speak.

On a crisp, cool morning in the month of April, John got word that he was being released from his contract. What a blow, having committed there for over fifteen years! So over the next ten days, John would receive communication from Highland about the details of his removal. He would also get communication from several schools that he had applied to in anticipation of the action taken by college officials at Highland. Would this be a replica of what happened before? John asked to himself. The timing of these correspondences between John as other schools that he applied to, as well as further actions taken by Highland on his behalf, would truly be remarkable!

John had already applied to two other schools earlier in the school year in anticipation that he, too, may be released from his current position. Both schools were in Colorado, and they were positions available in the area of language arts. Hooray! They were places where he would get a position that was similar to his position at Highland. And he would be close to the mountains! But John had gotten very frustrated with both of these schools being indecisive about affirming their decision to grant him a position at their school.

The other school that John had applied to was Washington Union in Northbridge, Kansas. The position here was the most promising to him. And after a few telephone interviews, they saw that he was a good fit at their school, so they offered him a contract for a position that was very similar to the one he has at Highland. There was a long deliberation process by which the officials at Washington Union came to a decision in hiring one of several individuals who had applied for the job, and John was that person. So time was growing short and the head of the English literature department at Washington felt pressured by the school's administration to make a decision. So the department head abided by the mandate of the university administration and made a final decision on a candidate. That candidate was John, and they offered a contract.

So at the last moment, John decided to give a verbal affirmation, to a Dr. Jones by phone, that he would be committed to accepting a position at Washington in his area of academic specialty. He did so truly at the last minute just before school closing for the day at about the five pm.

There was one problem with the whole situation, and that was that John did not really want to go to Kansas! He acted based upon fear that he would not be hired at one of the Colorado schools, where he really wanted to go. He had adjusted himself to the rural lifestyle present in Mansfield, working at Highland and of course, there were mountains there for his snow hiking excursions! In Kansas, there was none of this! Kansas is a part of the vast plains region in the midsection of the country where there are very few trees, and in some areas of the region, it is treeless, with only high grasses typical of what is technically called the prairie. So there was much agony and a careful thought process going into this decision. The next few days, coupled with what had transpired over the past two days, was a period of precision in the timing of events relating to John's potential move to his new position in Kansas.

John is a traditionalist. It takes a while for him to catch up with the modern technologies of the day. His nieces and nephews would tease him about being old fashioned and not being in step with all the modern gadgets. For example, it was only a day before he accepted the position in Kansas that he bought his first cell phone. The timing was great for this purchase because he thought long and hard about the decision he had made to go to Kansas for his new position. He really did not want go, but it was a good position and the people there seemed to really look forward to having him in their department.

That evening, John finally got a chance to get his mail when he arrived at home. To his surprise, he found a letter in his mailbox from the central administration at Highland.

And this letter was sent special delivery, and it stated that they wanted to give him another interview regarding his status at the school. Interestingly enough, only two days earlier, John learned that a head administrator at Highland, Dr. Strange, had submitted his resignation. Dr. Strange happened to be the main advocate of John's position being removed or liquidated at the school, which in effect meant that John would have no courses in which to teach or program to manage. It was unknown to John as to whether Dr. Strange had a personal vendetta against him, which may have led to his decision to terminate his program. But wherever the reason was, Dr. Strange was suddenly gone, which apparently opened up the door for John to be reconsidered with respect to his program continuing and therefore him continuing to work at the school.

John thought very hard about all these things after he received his letter from the Highland administration and therefore had renewed hope that he would continue his work at the college.

And hooray for the postal service! John thought. But there was a catch. John had already called the school in Kansas indicating that he would accept a verbal offer for a position at Washington, the position he accepted just as the five pm deadline approached! *Good timin'* so he thought. But he realized that he'd much rather remain at Highland than to move to Kansas where he was sure it would be a good position but without all of the natural benefits of a mountain environment that he loved, where he could enjoy his snow hiking hobby. Besides, he liked it at Highland very much. As an extra deterrent from wanting to move to Kansas, Washington is location not very far from Kansas

City, a large metropolitan area, and John is not fond of big cities!

The problem now confronting John was this: How would he contact the Kansas school that he verbally agreed to accept their offer of a position? How would he contact the department head, Dr. Jones, that he had talked to earlier and who had offered him the position? Fortunately, John remembered that Dr. Jones' phone number had been saved into his cell phone, the phone that he had purchase just a day earlier! Again, good timin'! At any rate, John decided to utilize his new technology and even though it was late in the evening, he decided to give Dr. Jones a call, on his cell phone no less!

So John called Dr. Jones and it was close to midnight! But John wanted to make sure that Washington would not go through with the verbal commitment he had made earlier to accept a position at the school. So when John called, Dr. Jones answered. John apologized that he was calling so late—so late, in fact, that the call came just prior to his retiring to bed, Dr. Jones said to John. "Again, good timin'! He wanted to explain what had happened earlier when he received the special delivery letter from Highland. So John nervously asked if Washington had processed the materials for his being hired based on his verbal commitment made earlier in the day. Dr. Jones indicated that no action had been taken. With that information, John thanked Dr. Jones for his offer but asked that his name be removed from consideration for the position.

For the first time in several days John had indicated that he did not get many good nights of sleep during this process; he had really been agonizing over a possible move to Kansas from the rural environment that he had come to love so much in New Hampshire.

Now John would wait for his next meeting with Highland. It would be determined whether his second interview would result in a reversal of the decision that was initially made to by Dr. Strange to eliminate the English literature course from the curriculum. John would have to depend on his conviction and focus his attention on the application of principles dear to him.

This story teaches us that sometimes we have to wait to obtain the things that we really want. This requires a belief that God will help us attain the things we desire if it is in His plan for us to have them (Proverbs 3:5). John then will have to wait, in quiet expectations for God's perfect will to be applied.

> *Trust in the Lord with all your heart, And lean not on your own understanding.*
>
> —Proverbs 3:5

CHANCE OCCURRENCE OR
DIVINE INTERVENTION?

3

Turn of Events

Being confident of this very thing, that He who has begun a good work in you will complete it until the day of Jesus Christ.

—Philippians 1:6

It had been only two and a half months since Al's wife, Paula, had passed, and during this period was a time of recovery. Al's house, situated on the rolling hills in Bismark, a city in the mountains of northeastern Tennessee, had been flooded with flowers and plants from the memorial service. *It was good to be home and get some rest,* Al thought.

Summers in Bismark are very warm, with temperatures during a typical day hovering around ninety degrees, and usually the humidity would be very high, a typical weather condition in the South during the summer months. But summertime is cherished because of the long winter, which sometimes starts as early as mid-October in the high elevations where Bismark is situated. The first snow usually starts a month later in mid to late November, typical for mountain environments in this region of the country; so summer is a time of preparation for the coming long winter season as well as it being a relaxation period from the previous winter.

Although painfully brief, the autumn time of year in Bismark is very pleasant, providing a nice, but quick, transition between summer and winter months. It was a time of music and cultural festivals. On a Friday afternoon after a day of doing chores around the house, Al wanted to relax. He would often window shop downtown and hang around at a newly built hotel for a while to read and sometimes enjoy a cup of coffee. There also was a library close by where he could linger and catch up on the news and surf the internet on computers that were readily available.

On this day however, it was different because it was the first weekend of September festivals at the end of Main Street on the downtown plaza. But Al was totally unaware of the festivities. After parking a block away from where the festival events were taking place, Al began to walk toward the plaza. Because he seldom came downtown on the weekends, he was surprised to see this special event going on. There were lots of people and several tents advertising everything from color portraits to food and drink. This part of Main Street had been converted into a plaza where special events such as festivals and concerts would occasionally take place.

As he continued to approach the Main Street area where the festival was occurring,he came up to the first of several tents that he saw. Being inquisitive, he stopped to ask the attendants about what the festival was all about since he had no knowledge of a special event being held downtown on this particular day. The festival happened to be the International Festival, the first of many festivals that occurred at that location in the city on weekends during the month of September.

Al later decided to do some research on all the other cultural events that were going to come to the city on weekends during the month. He found that on subsequent weekends in the month of September other festivals that were planned included the African-American Festival, the Bluegrass Festival, and the German festival. All these events would cater to various cultures in which Al found to be very interesting. To help during a transitional period in his life, Al looked forward to attending the remainder of this festival during the upcoming weekend as well as to experience the other festivals scheduled for Main Street during the month. So before the end of September, Al got a good dose of various cultures by attending festivals on the weekend. After all, it was something to occupy his time as he continued the grieving process.

Shortly after entering the plaza where the International Festival was taking place, Al noticed a banner attached to a table where various pamphlets and brochures were being displayed as well as various other materials. It was obvious that some college or university was being advertised and promoted. As he got closer to the tent, he saw that it was Southeast Community College. So, being interested in having additional things to do in his recent retirement, as well as to help fill a void since the passing of Paula, he decided to come to the table and review the various materials being advertised. He soon would inquire about possible job opportunities at this school.

After reviewing some of the materials on the table, Al saw the individuals who were promoting what he had seen on the banner and the information in the various brochures that were distributed on the table. As Al reviewed the materials, there were two ladies standing and talking with any one passing by who would stop and inquire about anything lying on the table. They were indicating what opportunities existed at the college for employment; there were materials for perspective students as well. Al learned that the school was located about thirty miles from where he lived in Bismark.

Soon Al began talking to one of the ladies. She began to give him more detailed information about the college, and he wanted to see what possibilities existed for gaining employment there. You see, Al had been a history instructor at a small college in Bismark before he retired just recently and was looking for other teaching opportunities in the area. He had considered possibly being a substitute teacher at the local high school, but his heart was really working with college students.

After a short conversation, Al found that the lady's name was Evelyn. Evelyn indicated that she, and her partner, Addie, were representing the school in the recruitment of students to their campus. Al indicated his desire to obtain a position at the school as a part-time instructor. As they continued to talk Evelyn indicated that one of the officials at her school had close ties to the school Al had recently retired from, City College. So, that acknowledgment sparked a lengthy conversation about this person, whose name was Fred. Evelyn talked about how Fred, in addition to his duties as an administrator at her school, was currently a state representative whose district included Bismark. Al would later find out that Fred was an alumnus of City College where he had been employed all those years, but they never crossed paths while they both were on the campus. Fred had since become a member of the board of trustees at the school and had occasionally conducted seminars there involving political issues.

Evelyn indicated that she too had been recently retired. She had been retired for only about six months, so, like Al, she was getting used to not having the commitment of going to work every day. Evelyn also indicated to Al that she had never participated in such an event as this and originally had no plans to attend and help the school in this event on this day. The school conducts this recruitment event each year at about the same time. While Evelyn did more than her share of work after hours for the school during her years as a full-time employee, she had never worked for the college in this event nor did she have any plans to do so! Evelyn figured that her commitment to the school was over after thirty years of service; she just wanted to enjoy the benefits of retired life!

While Evelyn was very reluctant to participate at her school's promotional event, she did so at the constant urging by her coworkers. She did not know what life-changing situation she would encounter! She would later become Al's friend and life partner! So, was it a mere coincidence that brought Al and Evelyn together at this event? The turn of events for both Al and Evelyn would start this weekend, and continue for the next several weeks. This seemed like anything but coincidental! They both would later realize that God was at work bringing them together at this time.

As they stood at the tent, Al and Evelyn continued to talk about the school where he had worked, but his focus was on the fact that he was searching for a part-time teaching position, possibly at Evelyn's place of work at Southeast Community College. Al gave her his full name for reference, Al Parker, and concluded his discussion with

Evelyn. He found her to be a very personable lady. He also found her to be quite attractive!

So Evelyn gave Al a phone number to call at the school to get more information, and he wrote the number down as well as Evelyn's cell number. He wanted to be able to contact her to let her know the results of his contacts with the college. His hope was that he be offered a job, and then he could call to thank Evelyn. Al was soon ready to leave the Southeastern Community College tent, so he then thanked Evelyn for her help and left to see more of the festival.

Two weeks had passed since Al last talked to Evelyn when they first met. During that period,he had made contact at the community college. He spent some time, at first with phone calls and later visits to the campus, trying to find the right person he needed to talk to about the part-time teaching position he desired. Al finally met with an administrative official who was in charge of new hires for the school. Unfortunately, Al was told that there were no positions available in his teaching area. He was disappointed to be sure; however, he was very appreciative of the attempt the lady he just met at trying to make him contacts at the school where she was employed.

Over the next two weeks, Al did not talk with Evelyn during this period. While Al was not interested in meeting another lady for companionship and certainly not for a relationship, he wanted to meet her again to thank her for giving him contacts at her school. Al tried to call Evelyn the week after they first met, but there was no answer. He was unsuccessful on two other calls he made to her that week. By the end of the second week after they had met, Al still had not heard from Evelyn, so he decided to try one last time to contact her, and, this time, he was successful. So as they talked for the first time in nearly two weeks, Evelyn said to Al that she had been busy preparing for a trip to Italy with a group of ladies. Al asked her if she would like to meet him in the lobby of the hotel downtown where the festival was occurring to share his appreciation for what she had done and to enjoy some of the festival together. This was the area near the tent where Al and Evelyn first met. Since it had been over two weeks since Al had first met Evelyn as she worked at the festival for the community college, he was somewhat surprised that she agreed to meet him.

After a day of doing chores around the house and errands about the city, Al eventually returned home to dress and prepare for the evening. He didn't know what to expect, but at least he could tell Evelyn how appreciative he was in her trying to help him make contacts at her school. Knowing that by the time he would meet her he would be hungry, he thought that going somewhere to have dinner would be a good way to finish his meeting with Evelyn on that day. So he made reservations at a restaurant near where the festival was going on. After completing some other errands, later that afternoon, Al was driving on one of the major streets in town and was getting ready to make a turn onto the Main Street, the same street where he first met Evelyn and where the International Festival was located. On this day, however, he thought that surely another festival would not be going on, but he had forgotten about all the festivals occurring on Main Street in September. So as he began to make the turn, he noticed all of Main Street was again occupied with people, tents, music, and everything associated with a major festival just like it had been two weeks earlier when he first met Evelyn. He was really surprised but then quickly realized that he had learned that the month had several cultural festivals going on. *Well, maybe this will be the last festival of the season,* Al thought. At any rate, his plan to have a quiet evening of conversation with Evelyn in the hotel lobby near where they first met two weeks earlier would be altered.

Seeing that another festival was going on and that he could not park on the Main Street near the hotel as he had planned, Al drove to one of the side streets and, fortunately, found a parking space. As before when he first met Evelyn, he got out of his car and began to walk to where the tent was when he first saw her. This happened to be near the hotel front entrance where Al suggested to Evelyn that they meet in the lobby as they had talked about earlier on the phone.

Since the crowd was so large, Al thought that instead of waiting for Evelyn in the hotel lobby as they had agreed, he decided to wait on a bench near the front of the hotel where they both could view the band playing on a nearby stage. Al said to himself that Evelyn would have a better chance of seeing him if he were to sit there outside the hotel but near the front entrance since there were so many people.

So there he sat and waited for Evelyn. Al had become increasingly pessimistic about Evelyn coming to meet him. Al thought that since Evelyn did not know him well, she simply wanted to avoid him. So he began to think that she never really wanted to meet him again. All of a sudden, Al got a glimpse of Evelyn standing near the front of the hotel looking to see if she could find him. Al noticed her and began to motion to get her attention. His first thought was that she did not see him, and he said to himself that she would probably get lost in the crowd and the evening would not go as planned. However, Evelyn did see Al and worked her way through the crowd and came over and sat with him. They talked a little and saw much of the concert together. Al had anticipated enjoying the concert with Evelyn for a short time, then, after about an hour he had planned to enjoy dinner at a local restaurant with Evelyn. To Evelyn's surprise, after the band had stopped playing and took a break for intermission, Al suggested that they go to this restaurant before it got too late. So again, to Al's surprise, she agreed so they went to the restaurant.

After navigating through the crowd and eventually reaching Al's car, they left the downtown area where the festival was occurring and took a short drive to the restaurant. Al had planned for the dinner and had made reservations earlier in the day, hoping that Evelyn would go along with the idea. It was a classy restaurant with an outdoor patio and covered dinner tables with candles. Al found that it had a nice rooftop bar for very causal dining and drinking. They would later go to this restaurant and lounge on the rooftop before the cold weather sat in. During the time they were eating Evelyn mentioned that she was looking forward to the next two weeks in Italy. She indicated that they still could call each other on a limited basis. This was a Saturday evening, so before Evelyn was to go away on her trip at the beginning of the following week, they found the time to attend a movie the next evening. Soon Evelyn would be ready to make her trip overseas. She knew that she had a new friend she could communicate with back home in the States while she was away in a foreign country. That's pretty cool, she thought.

Well, for the next two weeks Al and Evelyn communicated by phone, usually every afternoon at about four p.m. in US East Coast time. With the time difference Evelyn actually made the call each day in the morning at about seven a.m. local time in Italy. Eventually, after about two weeks, Evelyn, with her group of ladies, made it back to the US.

Upon Evelyn's return, she and Al resumed seeing each other and enjoyed each other's company. They talked about many different things, including her past relationships and how they did not materialize as she would have wanted. She believed that God meant for men and women to have committed relationships ultimately ending in marriage, but in her experience, she found that it was extremely difficult to find a man willing to have a committed relationship. They also talked about their religious beliefs and how she decided to not worry about finding a committed relationship unless God would intervene in her situation. She indicated that she was perfectly at peace in going the glory not having that desire fulfilled, trusting that God always would do what is best for her. She said that a very active life kept her busy with friends and relatives. She especially looked forward to visiting her brother in Alabama for Thanksgiving dinner during the upcoming holiday season, as she had done for years before. Al mentioned to Evelyn during their conversation that he enjoyed her company very much, and her feeling toward Al was mutual. But at the time, Al had no intentions of developing another long-term committed relationship. He simply looked forward to enjoying life being single again. Eventually, they would have a meeting of the minds and agreed to *go with the flow,* so to speak, as far as their relationship was concerned.

During this time Al introduced Evelyn to his daughters, Tonya and Dee. During this early period however, Evelyn didn't see much of them. At that time they weren't overly interested in seeing another lady in their father's life, not after only a few months of losing their mother. But they were respectful of her and recognized some of the similarities between Evelyn and their mother. Tonya especially was focusd on getting her life together with her new job and grieving in her own way. She indicated that a six-month period of refocusing her life would complete the grieving process and that she could move on with her life and would continue to grow as a person, as this is what she felt her mother would have wanted. Later, Tonya as well as her sister Dee would become more interactive with Evelyn. She realized that her mother is now in a good place at home in a place of joy and peace (Revelation 2:7). So both Tonya and Dee liked Evelyn, and they enjoyed her being with their father. They often would go out for dinner together, and later, after Evelyn and Al were married, they would come to their house and have Sunday dinner as well as meet on other occasions. It certainly became a family affair!

As the fall season wore on the issue came up involving Thanksgiving in a few weeks. Professionals involved in grief management indicate that major holidays after a spouse's passing is especially difficult for the surviving spouse. This is because the previous holidays that were spent with that person must now be spent without them, often alone. So times during formal events and holidays are difficult. So Al did not look forward to the upcoming holidays. However, he had planned to attend the annual family gathering for Thanksgiving as he had done with Paula for years before. After all, his two daughters were going to be there, and Al wanted to be with them, realizing that it still would not be the same without Paula.

Something very interesting happened the Sunday prior to Thanksgiving that week. Al received a call from his brother-in-law, Ray, who lived in Cedar Rapids, Florida, a small town near the Florida/Georgia border. Al was with his two daughters and Evelyn at a local restaurant at the time, having dinner together on a Sunday evening. Ray called to let Al know that his sister had a brief hospital stay and was now recuperating at home. Ray gave Al some of the essentials of the situation and assured him that it would be fine for him to call back to give him more details about his sister's condition. So Al said to Ray to call back after he return home and that he would talk to him at length about his sister and what she was going through. Al did not want to take the time then to talk to get all of the details that he wanted. So he said to him to call back tomorrow when he could talk longer.

So Ray called back but not until two days later, on a Tuesday, and talked in detail about Al's sister's condition. He said that his sister Janice had an accident while jogging and had fallen down on her side. Al was told by his brother-in-law that Janice had gone to the doctor and said that she could have a minor head injury. It didn't sound very good. He suggested that Al should pay her a visit to get more details about her injury directly from his sister and to personally evaluate her overall health.

So for the following day, the Wednesday before Thanksgiving, Al pondered the thought of staying home and going to Thanksgiving dinner with his daughters as he had years before with Paula. He also had this option of traveling to Alabama with Evelyn to have Thanksgiving dinner at her brother's house. Al was concerned about Evelyn's eight hour drive alone to Alabama for her brother's family Thanksgiving dinner, although it had been something that Evelyn had been accustomed to doing, making the trip alone every year for the past fifteen years. So trusting Evelyn's judgment and confidence in making such a long drive, Al thought very seriously about remaining in Tennessee to go to be with his daughters at Paula's family for Thanksgiving dinner but would call Evelyn on a frequent basis as she traveled on the road to Alabama, maybe every half hour or so to make sure she was OK while making the trip.

All during this time Al continued to think about his sister's health which caused him some concern. After considerable thought, he decided to go with Evelyn, to help her drive to her brother's house, and have Thanksgiving dinner there instead of being with his daughters in Tennessee. He reasoned that he and Evelyn would stay overnight at her brother's house then leave early the next morning to travel to Florida to see his sister, Janice. His thinking was that he would then ask Evelyn if she would go along with such an idea. Hopefully, Al reasoned, his new friend, Evelyn, would agree.

So Evelyn would go along with the scheme Al had decided on, and he explained to her the situation as his sister's husband explained it to him; and that was his sister was not in good condition. It would be only a three hour drive from Evelyn's brother's house in Alabama to Al's sister's house in Florida. So off they went from Tennessee early the next morning and after a long drive Al and Evelyn would finally arrived at her brother's house by mid afternoon and ready to partake in a nice Thanksgiving meal.

Thanksgiving dinner was grand! Evelyn's brother Denny and his wife, Tina, made Al feel right at home on his first visit. Tina had prepared an assortment of dishes, including the standard offering of stuffed turkey, collard greens, and cranberry sauce. Speaking of cranberry sauce, Tina would also prepare cranberry beans that everyone loved. People would ask for the recipe, but she seldom gives the secret ingredients. At any rate, after a day of festive socializing with friends and relatives, including eating, football, and giving thanks, everyone retired for the night and anticipated the first day of Christmas shopping the next day on Black Friday. But Al and Evelyn had other plans for that day because they had decided to travel to Florida to visit Al's sister Janice.

So early the next morning Al and Evelyn got up, had a quick breakfast, including a brisk cup of strong coffee that Denny had prepared, and then were off headed for Cedar Rapids to see his sister. Upon arrival at his sister's house, Al found Janice to be reasonably well as she was recovering nicely from her jogging accident. After arriving in Florida, Al reasoned, he would check on his sister, to evaluate her health condition and return to Evelyn's brother's house and stay overnight before heading back home the next day. So after staying overnight at his sister's house, Al and Evelyn got up the next morning and drove back to her brother's house in Alabama. They stayed there until the next morning when Al and Evelyn got up from bed and had a little breakfast before taking off for home. They would then drive the next eight hours back to Tennessee where they both lived. This would be quite a bit of driving on the road during the Thanksgiving holiday. But it would be a way of killing two birds with one stone, so to speak! That is the say, Al could help Evelyn with her Thanksgiving trip driving while at the same time check on his sister. The one down side was that Al would not be with his daughters at Thanksgiving back in Tennessee.

The next holiday coming up for Al was Christmas. Christmas was always a fun time of year, despite the hustle and bustle associated with it. In past years at that time, Al was usually busy putting up decorations at his house. It was always a lot of work for him, but at the same time, it was an exciting part of the holiday spirit of the season. The strange thing is that afterward, Al really appreciated what he had accomplished, whether it was putting up candlelights in the windows, wreaths on the doors, or especially the Christmas tree in the living room. Of course, there was the shopping and sometimes sifting through the snow that had accumulated by that time of year. Many times, it was an indication of the long winter that was to come. The crowded retail stores and shopping malls at Christmas time beamed with music like "Jungle Bells" and "White Christmas." By the time, everyone that had come home after work in December night would have fallen, and all the glitter of the Christmas season was on display! There were decorations everywhere.

With most people, it is a joyous time of year although sometimes the true meaning of the holiday gets lost in all the commercialization involved! That part of the season will probably never change, but at least most people seem to express goodwill as much as possible. Of course, like Al, Christmas to some might not be as joyous as it could be, whether it is because of the loss of a loved one, being unemployed, or simply being homeless. But the Parkers were well aware that the real purpose of the holiday was in the celebration of Jesus's birthday, and each member recognized this fact in their own way.

Over the years, the family was busy buying gifts for one another, but it always seemed that at least one person would find out what their present was. But everyone made sure that they place their gift in the house where no one would find it so that it could be a total surprise to the recipient on Christmas morning. So everyone was always curious as to where a gift may be hidden in the house to be opened on Christmas day. Was it in a closet, under a bed, behind a couch, or some other location that no one would suspect that a gift would be located? But within a week of the big day, gifts would have been wrapped and placed under the Christmas tree or beside the fireplace. Christmas Eve was always exciting with small kids believing that Santa would somehow travel from the North Pole through the frigid, snowy sky only to land on a snow-covered roof to descend down a chimney to leave a bag filled with gifts inside. Of course, everyone would be asleep late that night, eagerly awaiting the surprises that were sure to come the next morning.

Everyone would have gotten up from bed by ten Christmas morning. They would have a quick breakfast and then were eager to see what presents they had received. They were all grateful for their presents, whether they knew about the gifts beforehand or not! It was the fun of the holiday season that really mattered. And after all, everyone all knew that the real reason for the season was the celebration of the birth of Christ.

Everyone, of course, had thoughts of Paula not being with them. Al's older daughter, Tonya, indicated that her grieving process would end only after six months after mommy's passing, which is a typical period of grief for the loss of a love one according to professionals. Interestingly, this year's Christmas day would be exactly six months after the time of Paula's passing, the time in which the Tonya indicated that her time of grieving would be over. The timing of this occurrence would prove to be very interesting and perhaps divinely orchestrated because it was on Christmas Day that Al, his two daughters, Tonya and Dee, and new friend, Evelyn, would spent Christmas together, with Tonya now being released from her self-imposed period of grieving!

The true blessing of this Christmas was that while it was the first one that Al had spent without Paula, Tonya and Dee were still together with father, as well as his new friend Evelyn. The Christmas holiday was enjoyable, though it was different than previous Christmas holidays. Al found that Evelyn had much in common with Paula, and the daughters said that their mom, remembering her strong character, would be fine with Evelyn coming into their lives because she reminded them so much of her. After all, their mother's main concern above all else was for the welfare of the children she brought into the world.

In the coming months, Al would often receive letters from the local hospice chapter indicating that they knew that he was grieving because for several months it can be very difficult for a surviving spouse. These types of letters continued and were more frequent in the next few weeks. Al began to be despondent with the continued communication of hospice with him because, while he missed his wife very much, he felt that letters portraying his despondency did not make matters better. Al and the kids understood that Paula had simply transitioned from this life to the next, and while it is natural for sadness to occur over the loss of a love one, if we are believers, we do have hope (Romans 8:24). But we have more than hope, we have the assurance that we will gain life eternal with God (Philippians 1:21).

After several weeks of continued communication from hospice, Al realized that they were correct in their approach to his situation. So Al had become much more understanding of the role of agencies like hospice, to comfort those who may be in need of their services. Grief, according to professionals in this area, is a natural progression for a surviving spouse.

Despite fine professional services such as agencies like hospice, professional grief management does not consider the possibility of a supernatural progression of events that could minimize or even eliminate the time of grief that a surviving love one might experience. God's intervention into the situation involving Al certainly provided a turn of events that transformed what should have been a period of grief and sorrow to one of peace and hope. That is what Evelyn provided not only in the life of Al, but also in the life of his daughters. So Al acknowledged that the grief he ordinarily would have experienced was limited not because of his strength, but because God had placed another person in his life, who was very similar to Paula, to help fill a void (Philippians 4:19). From that point on Al realized that it was not by his strength that he was so content in the face of adversity, but it was by God's favor that provided him a blessing that would make life's journey a little easier. But God was not interested in simply making life easier for Al. His perfect will was to complete His work in Al's life (Philippians 1:6). For Al, that life meant a transition from one piece of glory in his first wife to a fulfillment of God's will in providing Evelyn as his new life partner. To God be the glory!

> *He who has an ear, let him hear what the Spirit says to the churches. To him who overcomes I will give to eat from the tree of life, which is in the midst of the Paradise of God.*
>
> —Revelation 2:7

> *For we were saved in this hope, but hope that is seen is not hope; for why does one still hope for what he sees?*
>
> —Romans 8:24

> *For to me, to live is Christ, and to die is gain.*
>
> —Philippians 1:21

> *And my God shall supply all your need according to His riches in glory by Christ Jesus.*
>
> —Philippians 4:19

> *Being confident of this very thing, that He who has begun a good work in you will complete it until the day of Jesus Christ.*
>
> —Philippians 1:6

SUPERNATURAL PROVISION

4

The Abysmal Swamp Experience

Now He who searches the hearts knows what the mind of the Spirit is because He makes intercession for the saints according to the will of God.

—Romans 8:27

Jack, Alice, and their three small girls would often take recreational trips together. Jack was employed in the athletic department at Elizabeth Town State University, a small institution on the northeastern coast of North Carolina. He received many "perks" on his job. Jack lived at least twenty minutes from his work where he traveled with his van, one of two vehicles the family had. Alice had her vehicle as well as she worked as a library technician at a local high school. She too had to travel at least twenty minutes to get from their house to her job. She also took her three girls to and from school. Benny was in the third grade and the twins, Mary and Monique were in the second grade. Needless to say the condition of the vehicles that Jack and Alice had was very important to them because they often had to take the girls to and from school, as well as to various other school functions, shopping, and to church.

Because of their modest income, the family rarely took long trips, but Jack, being in the athletic department at his school, usually attended the annual central basketball tournament at the end of each basketball season. So near the end of the basketball season and the beginning of the tournament Jack and Alice started to plan their trip. They had planned to stay overnight for three nights at the hotel which served as the headquarters for their school. It was conveniently located on the campus not far from the arena where the games would be played. There were seven other schools that participated in the tournament. The trip from their house to the arena where the tournament was being played was about an hour away in Norfolk, Virginia. The end of the basketball season was usually at the end of February. This time of year was very cold and sometimes unpredictable. For example, sometimes the weather would be very mild but usually this time of year was known to have lots of snow and blustery conditions.

A few weeks before the tournament the forecast called for below normal temperatures with strong likelihood of a wintery mix, meaning snow, sleet, frozen rain, and even wind. Sure enough, two days from the time in which they would depart for the tournament the weather turned for the worst with lots of freezing rain and snow in the forecast for the weekend. What made things worst was that the road between their home and the tournament site was not a very good one. It had only two lanes and was very narrow; also, there was no place to pull over to the side if there had been an emergency. Beyond the road on both sides were mostly brush, swamp, and trees scattered not to far from the roadway. Jack had made a commitment to being present for a banquet on the Saturday, the last day of the tournament, and therefore decided to drive the large van the family had to the tournament. It proved to be an eventful trip to say the least.

The morning of the last day of the tournament Jack and Alice spent packing and getting ready for their return trip home later that night after the evening's events, which included the banquet Jack had committed to. Two games were played that night; the first game was at five and the second game was at seven thirty. After the second game, which would end about ten, the closing banquet was scheduled to start at about ten thirty. After an hour at the banquet Jack and Alice had anticipated heading back home with the kids.

At the close of the banquet, Jack and Alice, with the kids, lingered around, talking and socializing with people they knew, not realizing how bad the weather was outside. Finally, they started back home at about eleven thirty, long after Jack had hoped to be on the road going home. Once they got started heading back home, Jack found that the roads were a mess, with ice and a heavy snowfall. It provided a beautiful wintry scene but the roads were treacherous. But they had made the decision to return home that night and so off they went on their journey back home.

When the family left the arena that night they were met with a cold winter wind and snowy conditions outside. Jack hoped that the one hour trip back home would be without a major problem. When they started out things seemed fine. His team had won the championship of the tournament! In addition, the banquet had been enjoyable as several players received plaques for their effort on the basketball court. Only the weather seemed not to cooperate to provide an enjoyable evening away from home. It took a long time for Jack to drive out of the parking lot in front of the arena because of the heavy traffic. Eventually, they were safely on the highway and the traffic became less and less congested.

Soon they would come to a very rural area between the tournament site and the family's home. It was a wilderness area called the Abysmal Swamp. The name was appropriate because this was a long stretch of narrow, winding roadway with very few areas you could pull over to the side only wooded, swampy areas were next to the road. Plus, it was now after midnight and it seemed like they were the only ones on the road.

The next sequence of events seemed to be very unusual. As Jack continued driving on this long, narrow snowy road after midnight, he had hoped that his vehicle would make it safely home. Being in the Abysmal Swamp was not especially safe, so a vehicle problem was something he did not want to think about. What made matters worst was that Jack had recently learned on the news that there possibly was an escape convict in the area. The person had reportedly committed several robberies and assaults in a small town nearby. Just as that peace of news pass through Jack's mind, he noticed that the "check engine" light on the van's dashboard lit up. Jack's heart began to skip a beat while he pondered what would happen if his wife and his children were stranded in the Abysmal Swamp because of vehicle problems. As Jack drove farther, the car began to slow down even as he pushed the gas pedal closer and closer to the floor of the vehicle. He realized that something serious was wrong with the van so he began to pray in silence.

Jack thought at that time his prayers were not heard because the van gradually came to a stop on this narrow road in the middle of the Abysmal Swamp. But then, the first of many blessings happened on the remainder of the trip. He and his family was able to pass through the forest to the safety of their home (Romans 8:27)! And this is how it happened: First, the van slowed down to a stop in one of the few available areas on the side of this road where a vehicle could come to and stop off the pavement onto a level area just to the side of the road. Jack guided his vehicle off the road to the level surface area without going into heavy brush or, worse, going into a swallow waterlogged ditch. Almost the entire distance from the tournament site on this particular road, there was hardly any area on the side where a vehicle could pull over safely off the road. Jack's van being off the road in its disabled state was important because it allowed his vehicle to be out of the path of oncoming vehicles. But as Jack's van slowed down and eventually came to a stop because it could not go any farther, it did so at one of the few places along the road where the vehicle could rest on level ground. So there they were: Jack, Alice, and the kids stranded on the side of a forested road after midnight with little or no traffic passing by.

The second blessing that happened to Jack and his family was that they were able to keep warm while waiting for someone to stop to help them to get home that night. This did not seem likely because as their van sat immobilized, only an occasional vehicle would pass them at this early hour in the morning on a snowy road in the forest. Only an occasional vehicle would pass them. This seemed to occur every ten minutes or so. Alice remained in the van and prayed that she and the kids would remain warm because the temperature dropped to below thirty degrees. Alice had included several blankets in the vehicle on their trip so they were able to wrap themselves up and keep reasonably warm.

In the meantime, Jack wondered what he could do to get the van started. Fortunately, the kids were sound asleep and did not recognize the danger.

Third, someone did eventually stop to give them some assistance. Jack got out of the vehicle and raised the hood to check the engine and found that there was nothing he could do to get the van started. He decided to remain outside the van to hopefully flag down a passing vehicle. Things did not look good because being after midnight in late winter and on a snowy night at that, things did not look promising for someone to pass them. And if they did stop would they help strangers? After ten minutes, a vehicle did pass, but did not stop, then after another five minutes, another vehicle passed. This time however, a few seconds after the vehicle passed Jack saw that the car was backing up. It backed up and continued past them moving in reverse, then the vehicle started to move up toward them until it stopped just behind Jack's strained van. Jack didn't know what to make of it, hoping that the person was there on a friendly basis and would be willing to help them. So as the person got out of his car, Jack saw that it was a middle aged man, and as the man got a little closer he asked Jack if he needed help. Jack said that he did and had his family inside the strained vehicle.

The man told Jack that as he passed them, he thought that the van was his friend's vehicle so his intentions were to stop and help his friend out. He said to Jack as he got closer to the strained vehicle he saw that it was not his friend's vehicle but that he was confronting a stranger. He told Jack that he was very apprehensive about stopping to help once he realized that it was not his friend's van. Like Jack, the stranger had heard earlier about a criminal being loose in the area, so he was not excited about meeting Jack, a stranger. Nonetheless, he presumed that the Jack posed no harm to him, so he eventually assisted the people who he thought needed his help. So as they talked a little more Jack confirmed that he did need help in getting home.

They made several additional attempts to start the van, but it still would not start. Then the stranger offered to take Jack and his wife and kids home, the remaining twenty miles to his house, in his station wagon. It turned out that the man lived in the same neighborhood as Jack.

Realizing that the helper was a genuinely nice person, Jack went over to tell Alice to wake the kids up. So Alice woke the kids up and they all got into the stranger's station wagon and he took them home, leaving the van on the side of the road. About one half hour later Jack, Alice and the kids were safely at home.

Jack thanked the stranger for his help. The next day Jack called a local towing company to notify them of the location of his disabled van. He would instruct them to take it to a local service shop.

With this ordeal over, Jack realized that through negative circumstances on his family's trip from the central tournament, sometimes it takes God's intervention to realize that His Spirit is always with us.

> *Now He who searches the hearts knows what the mind of the Spirit is because He makes intercession for the saints according to the will of God.*
>
> —Romans 8:27

DO YOU BELIEVE THIS?

5

Going Home

And whoever lives and believes in Me
shall never die. Do you believe this?

—John 11:26

The Parkers were always a close family, but because of circumstances relating to job location Al ended up working out-of-town and away from wife Jean and daughters Sonya and Bee. Jean had just retired from a state government position in Columbia,South Carolina, where she worked to help reach thirty years of state employment. This was a goal of hers because retirement from the state government, for those who could achieve it, provide many useful benefits.

When not working part-time as a substitute teacher in local elementary schools, Jean was usually at home doing chores or browsing about in the community. She also cared for her two pet dogs, Dinky and Goby, and they kept her busy with feedings, walking, and other responsibilities of their care. Dinky was actually daughter Sonya's dog, but it became difficult for her to care for him, being that she lived in a condo, so she gave him to her parents to keep. He was just a little dog, brown and furry with big bulging eyes that often wondered to and fro. He was quiet most of the time, but when he was smaller, he managed to bite everyone in the household, but they were small bites that didn't have that much effect. Goby was given to them by Jean's sister, and she just like to eat a lot. So both dogs became a part of the Parker household and were precious to Jean, especially when Al was out of town at work. Al worked for twenty-nine years as a chef for one of the larger restaurants in Charleston, which is about three hours away from Columbia.

Sonya and Bee lived in the same city as Jean where both worked as accountants: Sonya worked at a local law firm, and Bee was in a similar position with the state government. One day Sonya called her father Al to let him know that he should call Jean as soon as possible because it was very important. Al quickly called home and Jean answered. Jean told Al she had visited the doctor's office earlier in the day and was told that she had severe anemia. Jean said it was recommended that she began regular visits to treat the situation. In response to this news, Al said he would be home that evening. Upon arriving home after a three-hour drive, he found Jean to be in a normal mood, as she was doing chores around the house.

So for the next few days things were quite normal at home; this included Al and Jean completing a number of chores mixed with periods of relaxation over the next several days. It was springtime when people in the neighborhood were active doing yard work, spring cleaning, and other chores getting ready for the upcoming summer. With regular everyday activities, there are challenges and issues to be confronted from time to time. One of these times was when Al and Jean took a visit to a local hardware store named The House Depot to shop for some plants. These stores are known to be so large that a person could easily get lost where it would be difficult get around and find what you want. At any rate, Jean needed to get some flowers to plant in the yard so she and Al took off for the local House Depot store. Once they arrived, Al remembered that he saw an advertisement about cooking grills being on sale that weekend. Al loved to grill out during the spring and summer, so he had drifted away from where Jean was and went to look at the grills that were available for sale.

In the meantime, after a long period of time considering all the types of flowers and plants that were available, Jean finally found the flowers she wanted and made a decision to purchase. But wait! She uttered. "Where is my husband?" Al was nowhere to be found. She needed him to help her take the plants to the vehicle. Jean seemed dismayed about Al not being there to help her because they had discussed what they were going to do before leaving home. Al did not have a cell phone at the time, so Jean became increasingly frustrated. Eventually, Al made his way back to where Jean was, but by that time, she had somehow gotten the plants into the car they were driving. So, needless to say, Al got a mouthful, so to speak, from Jean as they headed back home! They made two more quick stops and then proceeded to the house.

Al and Jean continued their normal routine for the next several weeks. This included shopping and eating out on occasion and attending a movie every now and then. Finally, Jean made her first scheduled visit to the doctor since her initial diagnosis. At that time she was given more details about future treatments. The doctor confirmed what he had told her earlier and gave a little more detail of her condition.

Soon Jean was given a scheduled of regular visits for treatments. At home she had a bounce in her step because of the apparent effectiveness of her treatments. She was very encouraged and grew more confident in working with her doctor. She trusted him, Dr. Zachary, and believed that he was doing the best for her. She would later find out that he was a Christian, who shared many of her beliefs. This made her even more comfortable with working with him. She would later tell him if her condition worsens to always be truthful with her. Jean realized, as she was taught by her pastor, that we are all in a transition in this present life. She knew that there will come a time when we will transition from this natural, physical life to one where we will be given new spiritual bodies at the return of Jesus to this earth! She firmly believed the Scripture that says that be absent from the body is to be present with the Lord. (2 Corinthians 5:8). So Jean's faith is what kept her so encouraged, plus because of her treatments, she was really feeling a lot better than before!

So as the days went by Jean got progressively stronger physically. One day Jean said to Al that "I bet you thought that I would not be feeling this good after what I've been though over the last several weeks!" Al noticed that Jean did look stronger. Things were looking very good for Jean, Al thought, despite her continued hospital visits, but he thought that it was important to continue with their normal activities so that her mind would be as strong as possible during her recovery.

When Al was away on his job in Charleston, one of Jean's daily rituals was walking the dogs around the neighborhood. She did this so that they could go out from their fenced backyard once a day as well as for them to do their business. It turned out to be relaxing to Jean, and besides, she knew that she needed some extra exercise. Doing regular exercise was important to Jean. So when she was not walking the dogs, she would walk about a quarter of a mile to the local park. There she would do a walk-jog routine, which usually meant about six lapses around the park for about two miles. She also occasionally played a little tennis with Al on a very nice tennis court in the park. Al would joke sometimes about the quality of Jean's tennis game because she would comment on her days on the tennis team in high school. "You are kidding!" Al would respond. But Jean would always play because of the exercise and not because she was so proficient in the sport. Let's face it, she had not played since high school. But it was a fun activity and plus it made her feel much better afterward.

Sometimes her nephews, Jon and Jake, would come over to hang out and play tennis with Al and Jean. Like Jean, Jake was a member of his high school tennis team and enjoyed playing Al because it was always difficult for Al to beat him. But Al just enjoyed the fun of the competition, and everyone got a thrill out of playing. On nice weather days, it was just a fun time being at the local park. Upon returning home tired and often hungry, Jean would prepare things like hotdogs and pizza and have refreshments to just chill out for a while. Eventually, the boys' father would pick them up, and another day's activity would soon be over. Beyond home activities, there were occasional trips to the beach, assemblies and conventions where believers gather, and music concert events. These were just some of the normal activities for Jean.

But normal to Jean also meant being sincere, a word she like using a lot. Being sincere and having godly wisdom meant being very honest with people and telling them exactly what she thought about a given thing or situation where appropriate. Her honesty was most evident with Al on various occasions when she thought that she needed to be (Proverbs 19:14). She would say things like, "These pants you're wearing look terrible on you, so you should throw them away!" She would continue to say, "I'm telling you this because no one else is going to tell you!" Al would think, *What?* "Throw them away?" he would usually respond. "But I like these pants!"

But on most occasions when they did not agree with one another, deep down inside, he knew that she was right! And you know what? Later on, more often than not, Al would learn that she was correct in her assessment on most issues. The moral of this situation is that it is usually those who love us the most and who are most concerned about our well-being who are usually most willing to be honest with us even if it means telling us something we don't want to hear, knowing that constructive criticism is always a benefit. Our heavenly Father is like that. While He gives us our desires if we pray and believe, He knows our gifts, and He's always most concerned about what is best for us whether we understand or feel comfortable with His actions or not (1 Corinthians 12:29-31).

As Jean was recovering from her illness, she continued to have a strong desire to have a day care for preschool children. She believed in fulfilling her dreams, with no excuses, and being sincere with her feelings and emotions. On one occasion, Al and Jean were riding in the city, and they saw some vacant property in a commercial area. Al mentioned to Jean that the site would be a good one for a fast-food restaurant and that it would do very well at that location. Jean retorted and asked Al the question, "Well then, why don't you start a business in that location? Don't wait for someone else to do it!" And she was quite serious in her response. Al never fulfilled that idea, but it was an indication of the faith Jean had not only in her ability to fulfill her dream of starting a day care but also in Al's ability to start a fast-food restaurant, if that was really what he wanted to do.

Jean firmly believed that anyone could do whatever they wanted to accomplish in life as long as they put God first, above spouse as well as above children, relatives, and friends (Joshua 1:3; Matthew 19:29). Her mentality on this issue was displayed one day when Al mentioned to her that one of his interests was in becoming a pilot and possibly owning a small airplane. What inspired him to try this was that he had a friend who worked at a small college in the city of his employment who had become a pilot. He even took a few flying lessons at the local airport in Charleston where Al had worked. Al, having a modest interest in flying, thought that he would try what his friend had done and began taking a few flying lessons himself. Well, long story short, the story connects to Jean in that Al had mentioned to her that when he completed his pilot training that he would fly solo to and from Charleston where he worked to his home in Columbia in his commute between the cities. He then asked her if she would fly with him once he received his flying license. To Al's surprise, she said yes! That she would fly with him! Well, Al never completed his pilot training, so he never knew whether Jean would follow through with her agreeing to fly with him alone in a plane! But it is an indication she believed that he could have done it successfully if he had wanted to, and she apparently would have then felt safe to fly alone with him! So along with the prospect of herself starting a business such as a day care, she also believed that Al could fulfill his desire whether it was being a pilot, a professor, an author, or a successful person in business. The key to all these big dreams, in Jean's estimation, was keeping God first and following His directions in your life.

Saying what could be, as Al had said to Jean, about the possibility of building a restaurant in a vacant lot or becoming a pilot, without actions, it didn't mean a whole lot in Jean's eyes. She believed in having faith but also believed works of service releases that faith. And to work means to put into action what you believe. To Jean, putting God first meant being active in prayer, Bible study, and adhering to the golden rule, so to speak, of helping and being a blessing to others, that is, putting into action what you know to be right or what you desire whether people recognize the actions as such or not. And the exciting thing is that God recognizes and rewards our sincere actions of service (1 Samuel 2:3). She constantly put this idea into practice as she regularly visited individuals who could not do for themselves, such as the elderly and those in hospitals and senior citizens facilities or nursing homes. Of course, she would also visit friends, relatives, and church members, especially those who found it difficult to get around.

As Jean was recuperating from her illness, she was focused on starting her day care business for preschool children. After all, her three sisters had become very successful in their day care businesses, and Jean thought that she could do the same now that she was retired from her state government job. And Jean loved children, especially preschoolers as well as elementary kids. Her love for children was manifested one time when she and Al took a course in foster care, anticipating that they might accept a child to care for now that their own kids were grown and out of the house. That idea never materialized. But Jean really loved caring for children.

Jean had the opportunity to work with children, lots of them, when she signed up to be a substitute teacher at several elementary schools in Columbia, and she enjoyed that very much. She had been placed in an automated system where she would be contacted the day before a teaching slot would become available. The slots often would become open because the regular teacher would call in to indicate that they would not work that day. Upon listening to the automated system, Jean could then either accept or reject the opportunity to sub for a teacher at a school where slots were available. It was a good situation, being able work with school children as she wanted. And usually, Jean would accepted a slot to sub for a teacher.

While she enjoyed her work as a substitute teacher, Jean's heart was in starting a day care for preschool children. So soon she would end her contract as a substitute teacher and focus her efforts on starting a day care business. Jean had no regrets about ending her time as a sub because she always had a habit of looking forward to the future and not looking backward to what has been. (Philippians 3:13; Luke 9:62). She believed that the purpose of looking forward was in setting goals then going about the business of trying to reach them (Philippians 3:14; Proverbs 4:25, 26).

So to reach her goal of starting a day care business, Jean began to acquire a lot of materials, including developing fancy business cards with the name for her new business,

Blooming Birds Day Care. She also had accumulated day care items, such as tables, chairs, and games, many from her sister's already established day care. The only thing that she needed now was a facility to start her new day care center. So the search was on to find a house for her impending new business!

Jean and Al began to look at several houses: most were older houses on the opposite side of the city from where they lived. They had planned to purchase a house they thought would be a good fit to start a center. But the area where they were searching for houses, to potentially be the home of Jean's day care, was some thirty minutes from their home. They did not realize it at the time, but it was a blessing not to have purchased a house for a day care that was located at such a long distance from their house, given the difficulty of going to and from the day care to conduct business on a daily basis. After several weeks of searching, the houses seemed adequate to meet Jean's needs for a center, but all of them needed extra work to bring them up to standard for a day care business. So a major drawback was that most of the houses they visited were too expensive.

One Saturday morning Jean and Al decided to go to the shopping center down the street from where they lived; it was only a ten minute drive from their home. About halfway to the shopping center they passed a small house that had a sign in the front yard indicating that it was for rent. So Al, knowing that he and Jean had looked for weeks for a place to have their center, saw an opportunity. It seemed that God had finally provided a breakthrough to allow Jean to have a facility to start her day care (Psalm 37:4)! At one point, she even considered using the garage of her house as the facility to start the business, but she knew that it meant adhering to certain home business laws, which would be difficult to get around come tax preparation time. But as far as looking for a facility outside of her home, Jean was at first concerned because all of the houses she had seen before were for sale. The house they saw on the way to the shopping center that day was for rent.

Jean agreed with Al to take a look at the house so they called the realtor. It was good that Jean and Al would not buy a house because that would signify a long-term commitment, and while Jean was very serious about starting her day care, she realized that at the beginning both she and Al were testing the waters, so to speak. One reason why they wanted to be deliberate in their entering the day care business was because they had been under a mountain of debt. However, recently they had been able to pay off most of their bills. Now for the first time in several years, Al had enough extra cash to do some things that he and Jean really wanted to do like going to the movies, eating out, and doing other recreational types of things that they had not been able to do before.

So as they would begin to start the day care, Jean would take care of all the expenses relating to her new facility. However, Al agreed to pay the rent for the house. It turned out that the amount of money required for the rent was about the same amount of extra cash that Al had accumulated on a monthly basis. The only bills they had now were basic items like mortgage payments and other essential household expenses.

So it was to Al at least a bittersweet situation financially. On the one hand, he would be able to take care of the rental payment each month without it being a huge burden since they had found a house that was conveniently located near their home and seemed to be an ideal situation for Jean's day care. But on the other hand, he would now not have much extra cash to do some of the fun, recreational things as before. But he and Jean understood the price of starting a new business, and they were more than willing to accept that responsibility. So with Jean's taking care of all the other expenses relating to the day to day operation of the center, they were ready to get their business started!

As Jean and Al began to get the rental house ready for day care, they had some maintenance to do. Fortunately, upon their initial inspection of the house, they found that it had just recently been painted, and a new carpet had been installed. In short, the house was in very good condition and needed almost no extra maintenance to bring it up to standard for the operation of a day care facility. Thank goodness! An extra bonus was that the yard surrounding the house was large and well kept, and Jean had envisioned play equipment for the kids in the spacious backyard. It was late fall when Jean and Al got the rental house and began preparing it for the day care. By November, the day care was open for business! Meanwhile, Jean was able to get three babies to care for.

Jean had been caring for her three babies, Sanderson, Safari, and Din, mainly by herself, since the day care opened in November. She would get up early in the morning to prepare the facility for the babies, and then after the parents dropping the kids off, would start the routine of doing all the things that new parents need to do to their babies: including feeding baby food and giving the milk bottle, playing with them, and putting them to sleep, which would not come until early afternoon. And, oh yea, the changing of diapers!

She went through this routine for the first few weeks after the day care first opened, and then Jean was able to get one of her nieces, Jill, to help her in running the day care. So they managed the day care quite well through the Thanksgiving and Christmas season. Al had returned to Charleston after spending a few days with Jean after her initial diagnosis. Despite being the long distance, Al was able to return home on Thursdays for a long weekend with Jean before going back to his job in Charleston early Tuesday mornings.

The time was January, and it was the first month that Al had been retired from his chef job, and he looked forward to, for the first time in years, sleeping late each morning. Prior to that time Jean was busy starting her day care. What was even better was that she was doing very well as she had stopped her weekly medical treatments, only taking prescribed medication to help sustain her body. What had helped quite a bit from the time she first started the day care, was assistance from her niece, who was not employed at the time and, therefore, had the time to help Jean at the day care. She came to the center on a fairly regular basis and helped with various chores. Jean's daughters could not help her very much because they were still working full time. They were able to help her, however, on a fairly regular basis during the Christmas season.

So Jean would make the short trip from her house to the day care every morning to work her new business. She would get up at five so she could dress and be at the day care by seven. Before long, Jean encouraged Al to get up with her to go over and help her prep the house for the babies that would soon to come. So Al would begin to get up with her and help prep the new facility. He would mainly vacuum the carpet and do other things to help her get the house ready for the babies.

The parents would leave their kids between seven thirty and eight in the morning each day, and Jean would make sure that they be active and well taken care of. She and Al would take them to the Harget department store, a short walk from the day care, at about ten to get away from the day care facility for a while. They would purchase odds and ends for the center; but it was just a relief to get out of the day care itself and to be refreshed. The babies, no doubt, enjoyed the excursion as well! Jean and Al had to prepare a triple deck stroller she had purchased earlier from a friend and tuck the kids in so that they were comfortable and snug. The babies, not being in the world very long, for they were less than six months old, were amazed at simple things, like vehicles passing and other people walking about. On one occasion as they went to the store, one of the kids was frightened to see a huge truck passing by on the street in front of the day care center. Of course, they were quickly comforted by Al and Jean, as well as by Jill when she was available to help. Daughter Sonya would take up that responsibility later. After about a half hour at the Harget store, the babies would be returned to the day care center.

Once they were back at the day care, the babies were soon to have lunch, and after that, usually, they were ready to take their afternoon nap at about two. On a good day, the babies would be asleep for about two hours. This would gave Jean and Al a chance to rest, eat lunch themselves, and do more planning for the remainder of the day and for the next day's activities at the center. To keep the babies asleep, however, things would have to be very quiet around the day care. It seemed as though the babies, though fast asleep, were very sensitive to any sounds. So Al and Jean, as well as Jill and Sonya when they were available to help, had to be very careful not to wake the kids up! Even a cough or sneeze could trigger at least one of the babies to toss and turn a little in their crib! The babies resting would give Jean an opportunity to sleep herself in a bedroom in the back of the house that had a king-size bed in it. When the babies awoke, they would be fed, and it was not too long after that when their parents would come back to the day care to pick their child up, usually by four thirty. Both Jean and Al would look forward to the babies being picked up and to going home themselves for dinner, resting, and getting ready for the next day at the day care.

This pattern continued throughout most of the winter, but by late February Jean had become increasingly tired of the daily responsibilities that the day care was placing on her. She really did need some help in caring of the babies. She had been able to get her niece to help her during the previous months before. But by during the early spring after the month of March had rolled around, Jean's niece had become employed full-time and could not help her on a regular basis as she had done before. Jean's answer would be in her daughter, Sonya.

Sonya had been working as an accountant at a private firm, where she had been on since she left college. She had a good salary, but there was a lot of responsibility and therefore a lot of stress associated with the job. So she was eager to give it up to get a similar position in a situation that was less stressful but with greater long-term benefits. So she applied for a state government position in hopes of making a lateral job transfer. As a result of her actions Sonya lost her accounting job that she had been on since college and had become among the unemployed! Jean's other daughter, Bee, already had an accountant position with the state. So now being out of work, Sonya was able to help her mother at the day care on a full-time basis. Praise the Lord! However, Sonya had her own challenges because she had become recently unemployed with no foreseeable source of income.

Over the next several weeks, during the months of March, April and May, Sonya worked full time at her mother's day care. Of course, Al helped her, as he did with Jean. But Sonya waited patiently for a response from the state government about the accountant position she had applied to. The competition for the position was very stiff as she continued to wait for a response. She remembered the scripture on the value of waiting on and trusting God that things will work out one way or the other! So in the meantime, being unemployed after being released from the job she had been on since she left college, she would often tell her parents in a joking fashion that she would sell her condo and move in with them to continue a sustainable lifestyle. But the important thing was that she was there, available to help her mother in the day care. This was significant because in the coming weeks, Jean would lack the stamina to operate the day care without help. So Sonya, who also loved to work with children, was there for her mother, doing the daily chores of running the day care. Jean would spend much of the time lying on the bed resting in the back bedroom while Sonya took care of the babies.

By the month of June Sonya had become one of the finalists for the position that she had applied for and was very pleased with the way things were going in her job prospects. In the meantime her mother was not feeling as well as before and finally realized she needed to go to the hospital for further tests.

At home, Jean considered getting a walker or a wheelchair but realized that their home was not made for wheelchair accommodations. On a Sunday evening, Jean convinced Al that she needed to go to the hospital. They packed some clothing and went to the local hospital where Jean had been receiving medical treatments. Jean had resumed her treatments about a month earlier, and when she arrived at the hospital that Sunday evening, she met with her doctors who did additional tests. Al, Sonya, and younger daughter, Bee, were all hopeful that after a short stay in the hospital and with treatments that Jean could go home and ponder opening another day care center. By this time, she had decided to close the day care she had operated since November and had informed the parents of her decision. She gave away the many items she had accumulated at the center, and Al had ended the lease on the rental house.

Two days passed with Jean in the hospital and having another physical examination on Tuesday. Early Wednesday morning, Jean's pastor had met with her and the daughters; he had conversation with them and prayed for a while before leaving for another appointment. Al arrived at the hospital later that morning and saw Jean. At that time, Al met with Sonya and Bee, who had stayed overnight. When the doctor returned to the room, he told Al, Sonya, and Bee that the anemia had become more severe and that they could no longer treat her. When the doctors gave this information, Al and his daughters cried because they realized that they could do nothing else for Jean.

Jean's doctor had informed Al and the daughters that Jean might not make the trip home if they decided to take her back where she lived. So the doctor said that the hospital was more than willing to keep Jean and to spare the family the expense and inconvenience of taking her back home. But Al and the daughters wanted Jean to be at home, if only for a little while. Nonetheless, the doctors encouraged the family to have Jean remain in the hospital. But Al and the two daughters decided if she was going to pass on then it would be better if she was at home. So later that afternoon Jean was taken back home.

Al had prepared their house earlier in the week based on instructions given by the local hospice, who had been working with the situation for the last few days, anticipating Jean's return to her home. By this time, Al had communicated with hospice to determine what kind of services they provide. One of the items that turned out to be very helpful that this group supplied was a small bed that could be lowered and raised for the convenience and comfort of Jean. Earlier in the day Al had moved the large king size bed that they kept in the master bedroom to the guest bedroom on the opposite end of the house; there was a smaller bed in the guest bedroom that Al had transferred to the master bedroom. He would sleep on this bed next to Jean that night. The daughters would sleep on the king size bed that Al had moved earlier into the guest bedroom on the opposite end of the house.

Sonya and Bee were over by about nine that night where they settled in the guest bedroom. After a long day they attempted to get as much rest as possible without much success. But eventually they would fall asleep and later that evening they started to make regular visits to the master bedroom to care for their mother. The first visit was at about eleven and they stayed for about ten minutes, rubbing their mother's forehead and caring for her; at this point Jean appeared to be in a deep sleep. After a few minutes of doing this, they returned to the guest bedroom to sleep a little. While the girls were sleeping Al, not being able to sleep much at all, would occasionally rub Jean's arm but she was unaware of and unresponsive to his actions as she was sound asleep. After a while the daughters returned to care for their mother again at about two in the morning. And, as before they cared for their mother for a few minutes then returned to the guest bedroom to sleep a little. They came back for a third and final time at about five, just prior to daybreak.

During these periodic visits by the daughters to the master bedroom to care for their mother, Al had been in the bedroom all during the night with Jean as he laid beside her. He noticed that as the night grew into the morning the length of time between her breaths was getting longer and longer. As he laid on his bed beside Jean during these early morning hours he thought that Jean's next breath could be her last. He then reasoned that if Jean were to pass on, then he would need to rush out of that room to wake his daughters up to let them know, something he did not want to do or look forward to doing.

But the way it turned out, Jean continued to breathe those long deep breaths as the daughters came into the room to care for their mother at about five. As they approached the narrow hallway leading to the bedroom where their mother laid, they heard her take unusually loud breaths, and once they entered the room Jean took about three more breaths with the third being her last, a breath she held the longest.

A major blessing at this point was that Jean's passing was very peaceful, an unexplainable peace that prevailed the room at that time. (Philippians 4:7). Scripture promises that for the believer, there is no pain in passing since the taste of death has been taken away (Matthew 16:28), and beyond that, no one has an idea of the good things that await all of us as believers (Romans 8:18). The good news is that the Holy Spirit has the power to reveal the mysteries of heaven to the believer (1 Corinthians 2:9, 10).

It was at the time of Jean's final transition when Al and the daughters were at their lowest point in this natural human experience when the Holy Spirit was there to comfort them. The Scripture says that when we are at our lowest point due to natural circumstances, we are encouraged to continue to be strong and confident because the Holy Spirit rises up to a greater level within us to help us overcome any situation that we are faced with (2 Corinthians 12:9–10)! So Jean's transition was peaceful based on her countenance at that time. Jean had certainly overcome all that she had been through, as she appeared to have peacefully fallen asleep with no apparent pain or displeasure.

In the past, the Parkers would attend church services, Bible classes, and conferences where believers would assemble. At those meetings, the family would become more familiar with the Word, but as with all believers, the real challenge was to apply spiritual knowledge gained to real-life circumstances. One of the things they were taught is that this natural life is not our home. But rather, having the Spirit residing within our physical bodies, we are guaranteed a spiritual body that will live long after the physical body dies. Revelation of these things led Al and daughters to internalize their feelings of grief and expressed only silent tears as Jean passed from this natural human existence to a supernatural, spiritual life that awaits all believers.

Shortly after Jean's passing the emotion of the moment gave way to the responsibilities that surviving family members are usually faced with after the passing of a love one. One of the things Al and the daughters had to do was to contact the local fire department to bring the coroner in to confirm what they already knew, and soon after that the local funeral director arrived to transport the body for final arrangements.

Al and the daughters spent the next few days planning for a service for Jean. Within two to three days they discussed how the final arrangements would be done. Then they went by the funeral home to make these arrangements discussing various details with the mortician. In the middle of this discussion, the older daughter Sonya, received a phone call. It was from the state agency she had applied to for the job she wanted to get, and she was told that she had been selected for the job. "What! I got the job?" Thought Sonya. What would ordinarily have been an exciting moment was much less so because it came on the same day that she was helping to finalize arrangements for her mother.

Despite the adversity, Sonya was able to conduct the business she had to complete in order to get the job she really wanted. No doubt that one reason she was able to continue was her remembering her mother's admonishment of both daughters, now being adults and having left home from the care of their parents, to become more independent and spend more time developing their own lives. They remember their mother saying there will come a time when your mother and father will not be there for you, so you will have to face the issues of life, not alone, but with God's guidance. This was certainly one of those times.

Although quite independent in their work careers, both daughters grew up even more with their experience with one of life's most trying of circumstances, the loss of a parent. As with Al, they had to composed themselves to plan for the memorial service, which was a rather peaceful ceremony celebrating Jean's natural life here on earth. While in our physical existence on the earth death will remain a mystery, and its sting is something we never get use to (1 Corinthians 15:56). But as with the sting of a bee, the hurt dissipates with time. And to the believer, death is only a transition into God's kingdom that is yet to come and, in a very real sense, is already within us (Psalm 145:13; Romans 14:17). *Life in the Spirit* reminds us of that kingdom. It is up to us to believe it (John 11:26).

> *We are confident, yes, well pleased rather to be absent from the body and to be present with the Lord.*
>
> —2 Corinthians 5:8

> *Houses and riches are an inheritance from fathers, But a prudent wife is from the Lord.*
>
> —Proverbs 19:14

> *Are all apostles? Are all prophets? Are all teachers? Are all workers of miracles? 30 Do all have gifts of healings? Do all speak with tongues? Do all interpret? 31 But earnestly desire the best gifts. And yet I will show you a more excellent way.*
>
> —1 Corinthians 12:29–31

> *Every place that the sole of your foot will tread upon, have I given to you, as I said Unto Moses.*
>
> —Joshua 1:3

And everyone who has left houses or brothers or sisters or father or mother or wife or children or lands, for My name's sake, shall receive a hundredfold, and inherit eternal life.

—Matthew 19:29

Talk no more so very proudly; let no arrogance come from your mouth, For the Lord is the God of knowledge; And by Him actions are weighed.

—1 Samuel 2:3

Brethern, I do not count myself to have apprehended; but one thing I do, forgetting those things which are behind and reaching forward to those things which are ahead.

—Philippians 3:13

But Jesus said to him, "No one, having put his hand to the plow, and looking back, is fit for the kingdom of God."

—Luke 9:62

I press toward the goal for the prize of the upward call of God in Christ Jesus.

—Philippians 3:14

Let your eyes look straight ahead, and your eyelids look right before you. 26 Ponder the path of your feet, and let all your ways be established.

—Proverbs 4:25–26

Delight yourself also in the Lord, and He shall give you the desires of your heart.

—Psalm 37:4

And the peace of God, which surpasses all understanding, will guard your hearts and minds through Christ Jesus.

—Philippians 4:7

Assuredly, I say to you, there are some standing here who shall not taste death till they see the Son of Man coming in His kingdom.

—Matthew 16:28

For I consider that the sufferings of this present time are not worthy to be compared with the glory which shall be revealed in us.

—Romans 8:18

But as it is written: "Eye has not seen, nor ear heard,
Nor have entered into the heart of man The things
which God has prepared for those who love Him." [10]*But*
God has revealed them to us through His Spirit. For the Spirit searches all things, yes, the deep things of God.

—1 Corinthians 2:9–10

And He said to me, "My grace is sufficient for you, for My strength is made perfect in weakness." Therefore most gladly I will rather boast in my infirmities, that
the power of Christ my rest upon me. [10]*Therefore I*
take pleasure in infirmities in reproaches, in needs, in persecutions, in distresses, for Christ's sake. For when I am weak, then I am strong.

—2 Corinthians 12:9–10

The sting of death is sin, and the strength of sin is the law.

—1 Corinthians 15:56

Your kingdom is an everlasting kingdom, And your dominion endures throughout all generations.

—Psalm 145:13

For the kingdom of God is not eating and drinking, but righteousness and peace and joy in the Holy Spirit.

—Romans 14:17

And whoever lives and believes in Me shall never die. Do you believe this?

—John 11:26

MIRACLES IN THE MOUNTAINS

6

Double Trouble

He shall call upon Me, and I will answer him;
I will be with him in trouble;
I will deliver him and honor him.

—Psalm 91:15

Joe is single and has a zest for life. He works as a high school teacher in Jacksonville, Florida. Joe travels a lot, particularly in the summer when school is out. "Thank heavens!" he says. Don't be mistaken; Joe loves his work, loves to teach, and genuinely loves the kids. But because of long days in the classroom and even longer nights when he is preparing for the next day, he just felt he needed a break. Joe is disciplined when it comes to studying his subject in which he was trained, which is geology.

He often attends workshops for the high school faculty designed to improve their classroom instruction. One day after lunch with some of his fellow teachers at a local restaurant, he returned to his office to find a brochure on his desk about an opportunity to participate in a summer program designed for faculty professional development. It was a ten-week program in Denver, Colorado. Wow! In Denver! Joe always dreamed of visiting Denver and going to some of the ski resorts in the nearby Rocky Mountains.

Joe also loved to study the geologic structure of the mountain landscape. What was even more exciting was that the workshop dealt with map making, and he loved playing with and studying maps. Joe went through the necessary application process, and he was accepted into the program!

So near the end of the spring semester at his high school, Joe began making plans for his trip. Having never been to Denver, Joe was naturally concerned about living accommodations. After doing his research on the various temporary housing possibilities in the Denver area, he finally found a place where he thought would be a good fit for him to stay over the course of ten weeks. So he reserved a rental house that he had been sent pictures of by a local realtor, and he liked what he saw. It was conveniently located across from a local park that was surrounded by a nice paved trail. It also had some grills scattered in the area where he could go out and picnic on the weekends as well as jog a little to keep in shape. He also learned that it was conveniently located only about ten miles from where he was to work. *Great,* Joe thought. So after some preparations for travel, like making sure his van was in tip-top shape, off he went!

It was a long eighteen hour journey from Florida to Colorado. Joe had just purchased the van so he was excited about his first long trip. Well, it wasn't really new it was a pre-owned vehicle but was a rather recent model, but it was in good running condition. It was a long trip starting out from Jacksonville on Interstate 10 going west toward New Orleans. Joe would be proud if his van would make the long trip without a hitch. He had several vehicles before he purchased the van. However, there were so many issues with all them. He felt frustrated so when he got the opportunity to buy a vehicle that he could really depend on, he jumped at the opportunity. Anyway, Joe started his trip and after a few hours into his trip, he arrived in New Orleans.

New Orleans, Louisiana! Joe had always wanted to visit the Crescent City, as it is called. But he never had an opportunity to visit because he knows no one there. So although it would be a brief stay, he was eager to visit some of the tourist attractions that he had always heard about. So prior to staying overnight at a local hotel, he made sure to visit some places that he had planned to go to in this city long before he departed his home in Jacksonville. He especially had a desire to go to some restaurant that served good old fashion southern Louisiana gumbo! He loved gumbo as well as other Cajun delicacies. He especially liked some of the dishes found in this city that you would never have an opportunity to partake in Jacksonville, like steamed as well as fried frog legs, alligator, and turtle meat, offerings that are very common at most restaurants. And what made the gumbo so delicious was that many of these delicacies could be found in the gumbo, together with turkey sausage, a very rich and spicy tomato sauce and pasta of some sort.

He stayed overnight in one of the lesser expensive hotels, only one block from Bourbon Street. And, oh yea, he went out that night on the popular street and survived the experience! He even drank a little beer in one of the local pubs, which he would do on occasion.

Joe got up the next morning and headed westward toward Colorado via northern Louisiana, where he ran into a storm. He could hardly see out his window! He could only see the faint appearance of the headlights of oncoming vehicles, some of which, like himself, had given up driving in those conditions and had pulled over to park on the side of the highway. He stopped under a bridge until the rain abated, then he continued driving until he eventually got to the Texas border. By then, the weather had cleared, and Joe continued through East Texas into Dallas.

From the Dallas-Fort Worth metro area, Joe then continued to drive in a northwestward direction toward the southern part of Colorado. After a quick overnight stay in a motel off of the main road just north of Amarillo, he started his drive through the vast southern area of the Great Plains, a region of the country that he had read and studied about in his college days. This region included the Texas panhandle and the extreme southwestern part of Oklahoma. While driving through the area, he recollected the portrayal of the *Wild Wild West* in old TV westerns like Wyatt Earpe and Rawhide, for those old enough to remember these shows back in the 1960s. Many of these old TV programs, however, are now in syndication for older viewers to recollect and for younger viewers to experience for the first time. In the movies, Clint Eastwood's *High Plains Drifter* comes to mind when thinking about the natural character of this region. But reading a book, listening to a professor talk about the region, or observing the region on a screen of some sort was nothing like experiencing firsthand the long and lonely drive through miles of a desert-like environment. One description that applies to the region is barren, and there are very few, if any, places to stop along the way to refresh.

The geography of this area is mostly desert and in some cases the climate is technically called Steppe, an area of no trees and only short grasses and a few brush due to the lack of rainfall. The area is also well known for its rattlesnake population. Some legend has it that some species of snake in the desert actually follows its prey, which may be bad news if you are confronted with one. So how would he deal with an emergency situation, like running out of gas or having car trouble in such a hostile environment? It was a troubling thought!

Because of these concerns, Joe stopped at one of the last service stations he would see for hundreds of miles in the barren desert environment that was before him after his brief overnight stay at the motel. Certainly, in addition to having a good meal, it was important that he fuel up his van before taking off into the wild blue yonder, so to speak. He also had a check of all the vital components of the vehicle, such as the engine and a check of the tires. With everything checking out fine with his vehicle, Joe felt comfortable in moving on toward his destination of Denver, which was still several hundred miles away!

Despite the potential concerns Joe faced on his trip, he continued and eventually he made it to Southern Colorado, only a few miles from his destination. Finally, this area had a few trees that the region farther south where he just came from did not have. Also, the landscape was not barren and in fact consisted of vast farmland where there were a few small towns and villages along the route. Soon Joe would arrive at his destination. Finally, he made it to Denver!

He marveled at the snowcapped mountains in the background of the Denver skyline in the foreground, just like he had seen on several pictures of this metropolis. Being from Florida, he could not identify with the snow being present anywhere in the mist of summer. But at such high elevations as in the Rocky Mountains, snow is quite common because, as Joe learned in the study of earth science, temperature rapidly decreases with increase in elevation. As the temperature goes down, with moisture present in the atmosphere, it is much more likely to have snow as a form of precipitation. While Joe knew about these facts, it was still very intriguing to be able to go skiing in the mist of summer, and he certainly was looking forward to that!

As Joe moved around the city for the first time, he eventually found the rental house that he had made arrangements to live in for his ten-week stay in the area. He was able to move into the house, and once he unpacked all his belongings, he would be ready to start his summer workshop.

After about a week in Denver,Joe decided it was time for some relaxation and travel to some of the places that he had always wanted to visit. He was especially excited about going to the Rocky Mountains and possibly experiencing some ski resorts in the region that he had read about in his preparation for being in this part of the country. By the third week of his stay in Denver,Joe had seen much of the city. He marveled at how clean the city was, especially the downtown area, given that it was a big metropolitan area. Anyway, on a Saturday morning, Joe had planned a trip to the mountains. He made sure the oil level on his van was okay and that he had enough fuel to make the day's trip. Joe was now ready for his excursion into the mountains, and off he went!

As a geologist Joe had always been interested in the mountains and how they were formed. So he knew about what was called the Continental Divide, a region in the mountains that have the highest elevations, which separates the North American continent east and west.

So instead of going to a ski resort as he had planned to do, he decided to do some research of the area and get information that he could take back to share with his high school students. Joe was very familiar with the geologic history of the area because of his academic studies. The snowy mountains at the top of the Divide not only provided great scenery, but also was significant concerning the way in which the continent had developed over the millions and millions of years in geologic time.

With respect to geologic history, in which Joe was very familiar with because of his academic studies, the snowy mountains at the top of the Divide resulted in a lot of melting snow during the spring. Melting snow at that time of year led to rivers and streams increasing their volume of running water from the region of the Divide farther downslope. So numerous rivers continue to flow at a greater volume and at a higher speed than usual down the eastern slopes of the Rockies, for example. Based on his study of the subject, Joe knew that these rivers flowing from the higher elevations to lower elevations farther east caused widespread erosion that helped to develop the Great Plains region.

On the flipside of the equation, local populations in lower lying areas would often experience serious flooding as a result of rising water levels and subsequent overflow of natural levees. This occurrence would happen each spring as the temperature starts to rise, melting the snow that had accumulated during the winter. Of course, the melted snow would become water that filled local rivers to the point of overflowing and subsequent flooding.

In a similar fashion, Joe knew that the rivers flowed down the Divide westward into the valleys of western Colorado and into the Great Basin of Nevada. This is an area of vast desert wasteland of the American southwest. With a knowledge of these technical aspects of the geologic history of the region, Joe looked forward to going back to his classroom in Florida and teaching students about what he had learned about the geology of the region.

As Joe continued his journey up to the Continental Divide, he had to travel on steep mountainsides where there were deep cliffs below. The scenery was great, deep with cliffs creating majestic views of the ravine below. Joe was not comfortable at all driving along these twisting narrow roads. Of course, the winding roads in the high mountains of the Rockies had guard rails to prevent vehicles from going over the edge in case of an accident or vehicle malfunction. Although the risk was minimal, given the guard rail protection and the presumption of motorists observing safety rules in driving in such a rugged environment, one false turn and you are tumbling down an embankment or, even worse, down a cliff! But Joe was slow and deliberate in his driving.

As he came around one of the many curves as he approached the Divide, he heard a strange noise. At first he thought that he had an engine problem, but as he continued, he determined that the engine was fine and that the noise was coming from someplace else. The noise grew louder. Finally Joe realized that the noise was coming from one of the rear wheels. It sounded like one of the bolts holding the tire in place on the axle had come apart and began rolling around in a wheel compartment area where the tire was fitted. All this time as the noise continued, Joe was driving his van, navigating up and down the mountains on the twisting narrow roads and around numerous curves with steep drops offs to the side of the road.

What made things more frightening was that there was no service station or rest area close by. He had reached a look-over spot just off the road where motorists could park and see for miles and miles over the deep canyons, valleys, and smaller mountain peaks in the distance. At that location, there was also an area where people could purchase refreshments and snacks before finishing the spectacular views and start heading back down the mountain very slowly. Joe had reached the Continental Divide, where the view was spectacular. But what was on the mind of Joe the most was if he could make it back down the mountain with his van in bad condition, with one of his rear wheels malfunctioning. Notwithstanding these thoughts, Joe said to himself, *I am at the top of the Continental Divide, and I am going to appreciate the spectacular view of snow-covered mountaintops and everything else that this scenery has to offer!* So he continued his leisurely activity atop the highest spot on the continent! At least for a little while!

Soon, however, Joe had to come to the realization that he had to get back down the mountains, with a vehicle he could only hope would make the several miles he had to travel back down, given the questions he had about the condition of the vehicle's real wheel. So once Joe felt satisfied that he had fulfilled a long desire of his to see the Rocky Mountains in all its natural majesty, he was left with the daunting task that faced him, and that was navigating his van down the mountain with only three good wheels on his vehicle. So Joe would soon leave the top of the Divide and head back down the mountains.

While driving very slowly, Joe continued to hear the noise. With every curve and downward slope of the road, Joe's heart would pump a little faster. But he kept his composure and was able to make it down the mountain safely. Eventually he was safely off the mountain and in an area where the road was finally on level ground without the curves and the cliffs he experienced just a few minutes earlier. By this time, he was able to find several service stations as well as other businesses. Of course, his first stop was to take his van to a repair shop to get the rear wheel on it serviced.

After a close inspection of the van's rear tires, the service station mechanic informed Joe that three of the five screw rods that hold the wheel in place on the axle had come off; only two of the five rods were left in place that held the tire assembly together and connected it to the rear axle. That is to say to keep the tire wheel on the axle. The mechanic informed Joe that eventually, the fourth rod would have worn off and the fifth probably would have too with additional driving of the van. So, had Joe continued driving much further with the rear wheel in that condition, there most likely would have been a catastrophe! Can you imagine? The van would then been in danger of the real possibility of one of the tires literally coming off the vehicle while Joe was driving! If that would have happened, then the van would have been left with only three wheels with the real possibility of one of the tires literally coming off of the vehicle while Joe was driving! This was not a good thought to Joe, thinking that this could have happened while he was driving on those narrow curving roads of the Rockies. *Coming down the mountain while losing a rear tire?* Joe thought. It is apparent that God favored Joe by allowing him to maneuver the van safely around and down the mountains under those road conditions despite the apparent problems with his rear wheel. A fatal accident was definitely a possibility under those conditions. What a sobering thought! This was not good news to Joe, thinking about what could have happened while he was driving on those narrow curving roads of the Rockies.

At the same time, he was thankful to God that he made it down that mountain! Coming down the mountain while losing a rear tire? How fortunate Joe was. He paused and meditated on how he believed that God had allowed his van to make it to the bottom of the mountain without a major accident that could have happened, and with His favor Joe was able to maneuver the van safely around and down the mountains. Given the condition of Joe's vehicle, a fatal accident was definitely a possibility, but apparently, it was not his time to pass on from this earth, and a long life of service lay ahead of him (Psalm 91:16).The Holy Spirit was certainly with him during this ordeal.

While Joe's van was being repaired, fortunately, the service shop was able to loan him a car until the wheel on his van could be repaired. It was a big transition from driving a large van to driving a much smaller vehicle, but Joe was thankful that he was having his rear wheel being repaired and that he could continue to travel back and forth from his rental house to his summer workshop where he was involved with mapping. Joe used the car for about two weeks while his van was being serviced. He had grown comfortable with driving the car. It was much easier for him to drive than was his van.

An extra benefit of having the car was that it was filled with gas! That was good because he drove the car to many other points of interests in Denver and the surrounding area without having to fill the gas tank himself. He would later fill the gas tank, however, prior to returning it. So Joe continued to drive the car to and from his rental house and summer job.

By the second week of Joe's driving the car, it began to be low on gas. It was on a Friday, and Joe was to return the car to the service shop on the following day, Saturday, when his van was ready to be picked up. Joe's thinking was that he could go without refilling the tank during his use of the car then on the Friday afternoon after getting off of his summer job, refill the tank before returning the car to the mechanic shop the next day. The problem was that by the time he left work, the gas level was very low. The situation was exacerbated by the fact that the traffic was heavy as he left work and began driving to the shop.

Joe was driving along in stop-and-go traffic on "E" level at this point! The sweat coming from Joe's brow was not just because of the heat that day but because of the fact that it was a real possibility that he could become stranded in the middle of heavy traffic with no foreseeable way out of his negative circumstance!

It was rush hour in Denver, and Joe was driving along in stop-and-go traffic on one of Denver's major thoroughfares going out of the city, a four-lane main artery from the city's downtown area to the southern suburbs. Well, Joe had very little gas in the tank by now, and he was in the middle of all this traffic! And the fuel gauge on the vehicle's dashboard was below the "E" level.

Joe's worst fears were realized when his car came to a gradual stop in the middle of traffic. Fortunately, he saw a gas station ahead of him but it was probably about a mile away. Joe thought to himself that this is the worst possible place to run out of gas; it was made even more frustrating with the tease of a service station just short distance away. So there Joe was, strained in the middle of one of Denver's busiest streets at rush hour. Interestingly two things happened at that point. First, the traffic was so heavy that the vehicles behind Joe came to a standstill. So at first, no one recognized the problem that Joe had because his vehicle, like everyone else on the road in that area, had come to a stop. So Joe had some time to figure out what his next move would be to try to get the gas he needed. Secondly, and more importantly, with all of the stop-and-go traffic and his gas needle already on empty, when the traffic was ready to inch forward again, Joe's car would not bulge. He was completely out of gas! With this situation, it gave Joe an opportunity to raise the hood of the car and to signal to other motorists that he was in trouble.

So there Joe was. He was in the middle of all of this traffic in Denver, Colorado, on a summer afternoon. Joe just stood next to his car, hood raised, and now unable to move and not knowing what to do next! With all of his problems going on at this point, Joe had the additional stress coming from having the embarrassment of holding up all that traffic as people were in a hurry to get home. People were blowing their horns and saying all kinds of nasty things at Joe. He thought about walking to the gas station he saw, but it was too far away. Besides, he did not have a gas container. Moreover, Joe wasn't sure the gas station had a container for him to take back to his car. On top of that, he thought that it might not be a good idea to leave the car in the middle of the road unattended.

The vehicles behind Joe had stopped moving not because of the traffic had come to a stop because of congestion, but vehicles had stopped moving in Joe's lane because of him! His car would not move because it was out of gas. Meanwhile, the traffic in the lanes other than the one Joe was in, at least, began to crawl forward a little.

Needless to say the motorists that were behind Joe became very frustrated. Just as Joe was receiving all of the verbal abuse from angry drivers behind him, he witnessed a truly remarkable blessing. About four cars behind Joe's car in the lane he was in was a station wagon that, like all of the vehicles in that lane that were behind Joe's car, had stopped moving. Suddenly, Joe saw a man that was in that station wagon get out of his vehicle, and walk toward him with a metal container in his hand. The man apparently saw that Joe had a problem with his vehicle, and decided to come to provide some help. The container the man was carrying seemed to be a gasoline container! As the man got nearer to Joe, he realized that it was in fact a gasoline container! "Thank God," Joe said to himself!

The man got nearer to Joe and by now, standing next to him, he began carrying on a conversation. The man said that he had seen Joe's car ahead of his station wagon and figured that he had some problem with his car. The man apparently noticed Joe's hood being raised. Not knowing what the problem was with Joe's vehicle, he sensed that the car he saw with the hood raised may need some gas to get restarted; fortunately, he had a five-gallon container filled with gasoline in the back of his station wagon. *What a revelation,* Joe thought to himself, not realizing at that point that God was working through this person to solve the problem that he had. So Joe confirmed to the stranger that he had run out of gas. The stranger was accurate in his guess as to what the problem was and proceeded to put the gas he had into Joe's fuel tank. After making sure Joe's car would start, the man returned to his station wagon, which by now, together with Joe's car, were the only vehicles in the lane where Joe had become stranded. By this time, the vehicles that were directly behind Joe had driven around his car and had left the scene, and the traffic had become much lighter by the time Joe was able to move his car.

Joe never figured out how the man knew that he had run out of gas, as there could have been other issues with Joe's vehicle other than the lack of fuel. Joe was just glad that the man apparently had a notion, a sense, as the man describe it, that Joe might need some gas! The Holy Spirit was really active that day (Psalm 91:15)! He was active through another person who was more than willing to provide the help that Joe desperately needed at that time; it shows that the spirit of a person can be a mirror of God's goodness (Proverbs 20:27). The stranger even remained with Joe until his vehicle had restarted.

The stranger certainly turned out to be a God send, an angel of mercy! (Exodus 23:20; Psalm 91:11; Hebrews 13:2). After that encounter with the stranger Joe was up and running again. By this time, all of the vehicles that were behind him had gone around him and had driven off. The traffic then was still slow but was fairly steady.

The stranger placed more than enough gas in the loaner car for Joe to drive it the short distance to that service station down the street. So once at the station, Joe filled up the tank with the gas. He was now able to return the loaner car to the service shop like he received it, filled with gas.

Eager to return the loaner car back to the service shop and pick up his van, Joe had gotten the gasoline he needed, but when he arrived at the shop, he found that it was closed for the day. So he drove the loaner car to his rental house later that evening and retired for the night. He was thankful that God had intervened in a truly desperate situation. The next day Joe returned the car to the service shop and got his van that had now been repaired. The rear wheel had now been made functional again as the tire was now well attached to the rear axle.

So in Joe's last few weeks in Denver, he continued to drive his van back and forth from his summer job to his rented house. Joe had no other problems with his tire wheel and axle after what he experienced in the mountains. Also, he always made sure that he had enough gas in his vehicle to get him to where he needed to go. After the workshop had concluded, Joe drove the van back to Florida from Colorado, and by the way, he did not stop in New Orleans on his way back home.

After Joe's ten-month stay in Denver, it turned out to be enjoyable despite the challenges that he had, both with his van as well as with the car that was loaned to him while his van was being repaired. Joe's double trouble on his summer excursion proved to be yet another opportunity for God to intervene in a person's negative situation and, in doing so, help to increase our faith even in the face of seemingly hopeless circumstances.

> *With long life I will satisfy him, And show him My salvation.*
>
> —Psalm 91:16

> *He shall call upon Me, and I will answer him; I will be with him in trouble; I will deliver him and honor him.*
>
> —Psalm 91:15

> *The spirit of a man is the lamp of the Lord. Searching all the inner depths of his heart.*
>
> —Proverbs 20:27

Behold I send an Angel before you to keep you in the way and to bring you into the place in which I have prepared.

—Exodus 23:20

For His shall give His angels charge over you. To keep you in all your ways.

—Psalm 91:11

Do not forget to entertain strangers, for by so doing some have unwittingly entertained angels.

—Hebrews 13:2

MY GRACE IS SUFFICIENT

7

Cliffhanger!

Do not be overcome by evil,
but overcome evil with good.

—Romans 12:21

Johnson and Shawn had been friends since their college days at City College. They decided to pursue post undergraduate study in seminary school. They had a rather typical college life starting as teenagers right out of high school. And with both being single, they enjoyed the college lifestyle. Girls, alcohol, and parties were all available to anyone who would have an interest. And many young men off to college for the first time have at least a modest interest in these things. Johnson and Shawn were no different. So both these young men did their share of being involved in the social scene on campus. This may seem unusual for two guys with a mentality for seminary school, but while they enjoyed college and living on a secular campus, they both had a hunger to work in the church and to serve others. But while enjoying college life, they managed to study as needed and get their assignments completed on time. The product of this focus on studies and not simply the social scene on campus resulted in both receiving good grades and forming a solid foundation for post undergraduate study at the seminary.

As both Johnson and Shawn were in a general science program they had thought about teaching at the college level for a career goal. However, deep down inside they realized a calling in their lives to do a work of service in the church, and they figured in what better way to accomplish this than to attend seminary school to increase their biblical knowledge and to apply what they may learn to help solve people's day to day problems and address their concerns. With this in mind, they wanted to prepare themselves as much as possible and therefore decided to enroll in seminary school for their post undergraduate studies. However, they decided to take different paths to their future studies. Johnson decided to enroll in Murray Theological Seminary, a rather small but prestigious school in the southwestern part of Colorado, not very far from his home in West Texas. On the other hand, Shawn decided to attend Union Seminary in Wayford, Tennessee. Shawn was from the small town of Bennings, a short drive from the Wayford campus. Their dream about having their own church was just getting started! And they were excited about a change in their lifestyle from their undergraduate days at City College.

Graduation from City College came and went for Johnson and Shawn. Now they were both eager to get on with their graduate studies. It was interesting that while Johnson and Shawn were similar in many ways, especially in their career aspirations, they constantly competed with one another, which may have been one of the reasons why Johnson and Shawn decided to attend separate seminary schools as they attempted to continue their education. Murray and Union were both very different from one another, which in a way, catered to both Johnson and

Shawn. Murray was an all-male school, and there was a major racing facility not far from Ft Meyers, a small military town in Southwestern Colorado. In contrast, Union was located in more of an urban setting not very far from Nashville, which is, of course, the country music capital of the US. So both Johnson and Shawn ended up going to places that were very much different from one another but catered to their personalities.

Johnson loved sports car racing, especially NASCAR. He traveled on occasion to watch the Grand Prix, which is a major event in auto racing each May in Johnson's hometown of Blair, Texas. While Shawn appreciated Johnson's passion with auto racing, his passion was with singing and listening to music. He once helped his father at a local radio station; his father had a career in announcing and broadcasting. He also collected numerous songs electronically and knew all the modern technologies that generated and managed music. Country music was a favorite of his, but he also appreciated classical music, as well as jazz and some R & B. Among his favorite artists in this area were Barry Manilow, Ramsey Lewis, and Kenny Rodgers. He especially liked the work of Burt Bacharach in his writing of many of Dionne Warwick's old hit songs. A favorite of his was "Don't Make Me Over" and "Walk on By." He also listened to songs written and performed by Stevie Wonder. On occasion he enjoyed listening to some of the old rock and roll artists like the Rolling Stones, Little Richard, and Cher. So, as you can see, Shawn had a wide range of musical interests.

Johnson and Shawn really appreciated being in each other's company despite their differences in personal interests as well as in their personalities. Johnson was loquacious while Shawn was more reserved and thoughtful. And they had a habit of competing with each other—from who could score the best on tests given in the classroom to who was able to get the most attractive girl on campus. One weekend Johnson agreed to visit Shawn at his home near where he went to school. They talked about some topics dear to both of them, especially their prospect of succeeding in seminary school. Among the things they enjoyed was going to national conferences relating to their areas of academic interests, which was general science at the time. Before the weekend was over, they had agreed to attend a national meeting in Philadelphia, in which the major topic of discussion was to be stress management in the science community. After visiting Shawn, Johnson returned to his home in Texas.

Several weeks had passed since Johnson and Shawn communicated after Johnson's short stay at Shawn's house. Eventually, they started to talk by phone about their impending trip to Philadelphia. So once they got the details of their trip together, Johnson took off from his home in Texas and once again drove the four and a half hours to Shawn's house in West Tennessee. The route that Johnson took as he traveled from his home in Texas on the way to Shawn's house included the Ozark Mountains in the southeastern part of Oklahoma. Johnson was from West Texas where there are few mountains but rather a mostly flat desert-like environment devoid of a rugged landscape and lush vegetation. So he really looked forward to this experience for the first time in his life, and that was going to a national science conference and enjoying the mountain landscape along the way. Besides, it was a way of preparing for the trip with Shawn to the science convention in Philadelphia because the only route between Shawn's house and the convention site was through the Appalachian Mountains.

He would arrive at Shawn's house, though unlike his previous visit, this time, he would not return to his home in Texas but would continue to Philadelphia with Shawn to attend the science conference. Johnson talked to Shawn about his experience going through the Ozarks, for he had always wanted to experience the mountains. The trip would prove to be very interesting for Johnson because growing up in West Texas he was far removed from a mountainous environment. All the unique elements of that environment would be new to Johnson, including curving roads, steep slopes as well as the weather condition, which often was inclement during the spring time of the year. While he traveled through the Ozarks on his way to Shawn's house, they were no match for the majestic Appalachians. It was not unusual for these mountains to have snow and freezing rain, which occurred often in winter, and especially at some of the higher elevations. This was something that Johnson never experienced in West Texas. As for the curvy roads and steep slopes, he did not care for them at all. To Johnson, it was simply an imposing physical environment that he was not accustomed to seeing in the Great Plains of West Texas. This region consisted of extremely flat terrain, and it lacked the lush-green vegetation often found in mountainous areas. In West Texas, you could see for miles and miles on the southern prairie, where there are very few trees to be seen, and only desert shrubs loosely blowing around on the seemingly endless dry landscape. Johnson was also very familiar with the dust storms that would crop up occasionally, in which hot, dusty conditions were common. No chance of seeing that in these mountains!

They thought about what would be the best route to take on the way to the meeting in Philadelphia, which was another four hours away. Since all available routes from Shawn's house to Philadelphia went through the Appalachians, they could not avoid the mountains on their trip. As they prepared for their trip from Shawn's house to Philadelphia, Johnson noticed that they would travel through the Appalachian Mountains of West Virginia. Shawn, being more familiar with this area, agreed that would be the best route to take. So they both began preparing for the trip; Johnson had already serviced his car, and it was now in good running condition. Shawn reasoned that Johnson would use his own car for the trip; Johnson would never think of using Shawn's vehicle because it was an older model, and he considered it to be too slow. They finally decided a preferred route, one that would at least be a major highway but would bypass what little population development there was in the region and hopefully make trip a little shorter.

Soon they would be off and running or off to the races, so to speak, to their conference in Philadelphia!

As Johnson and Shawn were making the long trip to Philadelphia, they had a great deal of time to think about different things. One of the things Shawn had on his mind was Johnson's interests in race cars. While Johnson and Shawn were good friends, Shawn had always wondered how Johnson would do as a race car driver, being that he was so interested in the sport. And while he had a big interest in auto racing, Johnson was more interested in watching it as a sporting event than actually racing himself. However, being close friends, Shawn often teased him a lot about his interest in auto racing. He would sometimes try to persuade Johnson to try his interest in real life, on the open highway. While Johnson never responded to Shawn's constant encouraging to do something he knew he should not do, he finally gave in and thought he would give it a try, he saw it as an opportunity to show him his driving skills on their way to the science meeting in Philadelphia.

A high pressure system dominated the weather over the entire route of their journey and it produced very clear, cool conditions. It was ideal for driving, especially through the mountains. Johnson would not get the inclement weather that he had expected; the weather forecast called for clear, calm conditions over the next several days. There were no complaints from Johnson however. This meant that he could drive a little faster through the mountains, and perhaps arrive at their destination a little earlier.

The car that they were driving to Philadelphia was a Ford Mustang, which was a very fast vehicle that first came on the scene in the mid 1960s. The maximum speed of a Mustang was in the area of 120 mph. Of course, no one drives at that speed, right? We all know that state and federal laws prohibit motorists from speeding, especially on local roads. After all, the highway patrol, especially in the state of Texas where Johnson was from, very often prosecuted violators. Johnson drove his car safely from Texas to Shawn's house, and he observed all of the laws of good, safe, vehicle management, including speed control!

As Johnson and Shawn continued on their way, they saw that it was getting late and therefore decided to stop for dinner at an Italian restaurant off of an exit just before entering the high mountains of West Virginia. After they had their meal, they decided to call it a day so they checked into a motel and retired for the evening. They had just arrived in the state of West Virginia.

They started out early the next morning, and after breakfast, they were on the road again. After riding a few miles, Shawn had grown a little bored from the long drive, and while the cliffs and distant ravines far beneath the road were majestic, much of the drive offered only a few road signs and the monotony of mountain landscapes to view. Besides, the drive through the mountains didn't offer Shawn the excitement that it did Johnson because he was so familiar with this environment. So he resorted to listening to a lot of music, Shawn's favorite hobby.

Though rather reserved in personality, Shawn saw an opportunity to play a trick on Johnson. It involved trying to get Johnson to race his car on the public roads of West Virginia, in the mountains no less! And while the highway patrol was more active on highways near local villages, many of the roads in the mountains were far removed from any development and where the patrol was very seldom seen. Shawn was more comfortable driving in the mountains than was Johnson. In Shawn's estimation, Johnson would have a clear path to try his craft of the love of auto racing on the open highway for what would take about an hour and a half drive through the mountains. And usually there is very little traffic on mountain roads.

Shawn really trusted Johnson as being a very good driver. While in the mountains, there were sharp curves and steep cliffs along much of the highway, but there were also stretches of road that are fairly straight where Shawn thought it would be safe driving at a high speed along these locations. The mountains of West Virginia were considerably higher and more majestic than those that Johnson was more familiar with in the Ozarks of Oklahoma. But with Johnson having an equally competitive nature in his spirit, he said that he would give Shawn the spin of his life! It would be a thrill of a lifetime!

So as they entered the highest portion of the mountains, the temperature had dropped some thirty degrees as they climbed into the peaks and canyons of the Appalachians. No problems yet. Just two days prior, they were driving in the relatively flat, sometimes rolling, plains of Tennessee, which is a part of the Mississippi Valley region west of the Appalachians. While roads in the Ozarks were narrow, Johnson noticed that roads in this mountain area were considerably wider although the elevation was much higher. In these mountains however, there was a need to have guard rails up on the side of the road in most places because of the steepness of the overhang beyond the road. There were cliffs that were just beyond the the guard rails that dropped into the ravine several hundred feet below. While there were trees and brush to buffer the fall of any vehicle that accidently went beyond the guard rail, the consequences of driving off road and into the ravine below would be probably fatal. But hopefully, the guard rails were firm enough to prevent such a mishap.

On one stretch of highway, as Johnson and Shawn continued their journey, the traffic was very light, and because of the wideness of the road, Shawn challenged Johnson to increase his speed from seventy five mph to eighty five, which would have been twenty mph beyond the posted speed limit of sixty-five! They had not seen any signs of patrolman in the area, so Johnson felt that he should give it a try. So he foolishly took Shawn up on his suggestion and began to increase his speed. Johnson was now speeding along a rather empty highway at this point at about eighty mph, and the rush that he got from it was intoxicating!

It felt like he had taken a drug and thought that doing a mere ten mph more than what he had been doing before would not present a big problem for him. So Johnson used this rationale to increase his speed up to ninety mph, then ninety-five, then briefly to a hundred. He knew that Shawn long ago had challenged him to go a hundred mph, and Johnson was thinking to himself that this is an opportunity to do that, being only five mph from his goal. Remember, Johnson and Shawn are law abiding citizens, except in this instance! Usually, they respect higher levels of authority. But as younger men in an exciting and adventurous part of life, taking risks is not a foreign idea, and they had the feeling that they could do no wrong. They simply did not care to acknowledge the potential danger that was in front of them.

Much of what led to Johnson's thinking at this point was that the mountain road they were on was relatively straight, without many curves, and it definitely was a rather wide road, not typical for such a mountainous area. This was not to mention that the downward slope of the road was not very dramatic for many, many miles. However, things were about to change in a drastic fashion as all of a sudden there was a significant drop in elevation in the area they were in, and the road began to have more curves, notwithstanding that the curves were not very sharp. Nonetheless, Johnson came to his senses and decided that he should slow down, especially after attaining a person goal of his to drive at a hundred mph. So Johnson began to slow down, still going well over ninety mph. For the first time in a while, Johnson began to be a little afraid of the circumstance that he put himself and Shawn into.

As Johnson drove through the mountains, it was a clear day and again there was very little traffic. Heck, even the cliffs beyond the guard rail on the edge of the road did not seem to be so imposing although he was slowly becoming more afraid of the predicament that they were in. Driving in the mountains is no picnic because you never know what's coming up next. Boulders and other huge rock have been known to tumble down the mountainside and onto the road in certain locations. An event that could close the road and prohibit any traffic to pass!

Johnson's confidence in the face of fear also was fueled by the fact that he had slowed down to what he thought was a manageable speed. So everything was still going smoothly, Johnson thought, but Shawn had fallen asleep shortly after he had told Shawn that he would meet the challenge. So Johnson decided that he could increase his speed again slightly, remembering that Shawn had challenged him to drive up to a hundred, which he did. But when he did it Shawn was asleep! Johnson felt that he had to prove what he had done when Shawn was awake.

As Johnson was going around a another sharp curve, he noticed the road ahead was surprisingly straight for a good distance so again, Johnson thought that this was an opportunity to meet challenge once more, of him going a hundred mph, and have Shawn, this time, witness it! So as Johnson increased his speed, he woke Shawn up. Now totally alert as he had just been taken out of his sleep, Shawn could not believe that Johnson was actually doing it! He was driving at a surprisingly high rate of speed at this point, over ninety! As Shawn continued to get more of a focus by becoming more alert from his sleep, he wondered if Johnson would actually try to speed along the mountains. Shawn, while startled momentarily, imagined the exhilaration Johnson felt and what race car drivers feel going at the same speed but on a legitimate racing track designed for cars running at speeds of over a hundred on a constant basis. But make no mistake, this wasn't a race track, it was simply an unusually straight stretch of road in the high mountains of the Appalachians. So as Johnson eventually sped to over a hundred, he saw a modest curve coming up and decided that should slow down a bit.

The safest way to slow down is to simply take your foot off of the gas pedal. But since he needed to apply some pressure on the brakes rather quickly to slow down at a speed that would not compromise the curve coming up, he did apply the brakes. Oh no! He didn't do that! But applying the brakes was necessary for the vehicle to make the curve in an upright position! Because of Johnson's action, the car went into a slight skid, then a major skid! Johnson's action accelerated the skid, and the car began to turn around. While still going well over seventy mph, the car continued in its skid, moving backward along the guard rail along a modest curve for several feet. And the guard rail over-hanged the cliff below, which extended downward for several hundred feet! As the vehicle continued its skid, it literally hanged along the rail for several yards with the steep cliff just beyond it! Johnson's life had flashed before his eyes, with him thinking that surely the likelihood of going over the guard rail into the ravine below is real a possibility. Shawn, on the other hand, was so shocked during the experience that he did not say a word, but appeared to be hypnotized! After what seemed to be several minutes, in actuality was only a few seconds it took the car to complete its skid; which ended only as a result of Johnson calmness of mind to gently steer the car around to the point where it began to move forward, not backward! So the car began to stablized into a forward moving position as it came completely out of its skid. No doubt, and ironically, Johnson's driving skills were put to the test, and probably helped him to avoid tragedy. Finally, they were now safely off of the guard rail and driving forward at a much lower rate of speed. At this point they had decreased their speed to a modest fifty five mph, which was now less than the posted sixty five mph limit.

Obviously, the whole experience was a daunting one for both Johnson and Shawn because they could see very clearly the ravine below as they skidded along the guard rail for several feet.

Fortunately, the railing was very sturdy, and the car did not strike the rail head-on but rather at an angle. It did cause a big streak mark on the side of the car that hit the rail. Also, there even was a small dent in the car caused by the impact of the initial striking of the rail. But this was insignificant compared to what could have happened if the car had gone off of the railing and into the ravine below.

Sometimes God's blessings happen when we ourselves are the cause of the problem we have (Romans 5:8; Isaiah 53:5; Romans 5:19, 20). Nonetheless, it is important to remember that God does give us grace to make it through some situations, like the one Johnson and Shawn found themselves in even though in many cases we are the cause of it. However, sometimes if we fall out of the perfect will that God has for us, He may not always intervene on our behalf! In some instances, for example, God may not help get us out of a jam that we may have placed ourselves in so that we can learn from our mistakes and avoid making them in the future (Hebrews 12:6)!

So sometimes a teachable lesson can help us avoid the same mistakes in the future. The best thing for us to do is to genuinely make an attempt to do what we believe is right in a given situation, knowing that He is there to help us if we fall short of His plan for us. Making wise decisions can then help us to stay out of trouble. We should pray for God's help in our making prudent choices on a daily basis and therefore avoid many of the issues that we may otherwise face. Thankfully, God is still there to help us if a need arises, and the Holy Spirit can help us make decisions consistent with God's plan for our lives.

So Johnson and Shawn continued what had been an eventful journey to their meeting in Philadelphia. They certainly had the experience of contributing to the conference in the area of stress management because they endured a real-life situation that was very stressful. And most importantly, having a strong foundation in biblical knowledge, they realized that they missed an opportunity to obey the Spirit that was within them (Romans 12:21). Johnson especially learned a valuable lesson that making unwise choices can lead to near tragic consequences. Johnson was now content in simply following secular laws involving highway safety and allowing the Spirit to work within him to accomplish this goal (Galatians 5:16; Philippians 3:14). He, as well as Shawn, also learned that it is best not only to observe civil statues but also divine laws in order to stay within the perfect will of God. So for the next few hours of their trip to their conference was without incidence.

We all can learn the value of making sound decisions, regardless of the circumstances, so that we continue to do what God expects of us. The unwise decisions that most of us make are not as obvious as the one Johnson made while driving recklessly on the highway, but we all make decisions in life that are not in our best interest. We can only pray that God will help us to make the correct choices that will benefit our lives.

> *But God demonstrates His own love toward us, in that while we were still sinners, Christ died for us.*
>
> —Romans 5:8

> *But He was wounded for our transgressions. He was bruised for our iniquities: The chastisement for our peace was upon Him. And by His stripes we are healed.*
>
> —Isaiah 53:5

> *For by one man's disobedience many were made sinners, so also by one Man's obedience many will be made righteous. 20Moreover the law entered that the offense might abound. But where sin abounded, grace abounded much more.*
>
> —Roman 5:19–20

> *For whom the Lord loves, He chastens, And scourges every son whom He receives.*
>
> —Hebrews 12:6

> *Do not be overcome by evil, but overcome evil with good.*
>
> —Romans 12:21

I say then: Walk in the Spirit, and you shall not fulfill the lust of the flesh.

—Galatians 5:16

I press toward the goal for the prize of the upward call of God in Christ Jesus.

—Philippians 3:14

RESPONDING TO THAT GENTLE VOICE WITHIN

8

A Rainy Night in Georgia

Watch and pray, lest you enter into temptation.
The spirit is indeed willing but the flesh is weak.

—Mark 14:38

It had been a rainy weekend in Augusta, Georgia due to Hurricane Alex, which dumped over fifteen inches of rain for the three days of the storm starting on Friday. It was early September and at this time of year it is common to have a hurricane come through and do extensive damage. At least during these types of storms there is time for a lot of preparation, unlike the unexpected nature of tornadoes, for example. As a result, the people in this city were well informed of the coming of Alex, and most were prepared. A major hurricane had been forecast for the area at least a week earlier when it hit. So most people in Augusta were at the local stores picking up supplies they would need for the storm. And the grocery stores had been depleted of essential items such as water, bread, and milk. People were encouraged to purchase as many canned goods as possible because meteorologists determined that the storm would last for at least three days and possibly longer. And who knows the length of time of the lingering effects of the storm.

Karen Tate had done her part in preparing for the storm, including the purchase of a generator in case of power outages for an extended period. Karen, however, was keenly aware of the risks associated with hurricanes in this part of the country, and southern Georgia had been hit before and had caused millions of dollars in damage associated with toppled structures, tree and power line damage, and flooding. So Karen and her husband, Ted, felt that they were ready for the storm. But the focus of this story is how the effects this storm would have on the life of Karen, Ted, and their two sons, Peter and Paul.

Karen and her family had just moved to Augusta where she taught at a small college in town, which was Augusta State College. She had been there only two years, obtaining a permanent position in the biology department at the school. However, she had not received the doctorate, which was a requirement for her to continue in that position. In the meantime, Ted had recently gotten a position on campus as a security officer.

Karen and family were faced with one of the most dangerous natural events in this part of the country. Hurricanes are known to cause a lot of widespread damage. Since Augusta is located on the coast, hurricanes can create what is called the "storm surge," a rush of ocean water from the nearby coastline where beaches can be inundated with ocean waves and then can travel for miles into low-lying coastal land areas. Of course, the high winds and heavy rainfall can make things a lot worse. In short, a hurricane can result in a lot of damage. One of the consequences of the storm at Karen's house was that a big pecan tree in her backyard had blown over and had to be removed. It was a mess all around.

Hurricanes are low-pressure systems and, in meteorological terms, are followed by extremely high pressure that produces fair, calm weather conditions. So by Monday morning, things had cleared up, and people everywhere seemed to be out removing debris that had been left by the storm. But as late morning gave way to early afternoon, then late afternoon, clouds began to return, and indeed the forecast called for more rain that night.

So apparently, Alex had not relinquished its grip on the area. You see, there are bans of rain and wind that come with a hurricane, and although most of the characteristics associated with the storm had passed by Monday, it had become fairly clear and calm during the early morning hours. But it was only a temporary condition because as the day progressed, more clouds arrived by early afternoon. Then by late afternoon, a band of clouds associated with the storm had thickened, and the chance of more rain had gone up. Shortly after that, by early evening, a remnant of the storm produced a steady rain in the area. At any rate, rain certainly was the last thing that the people of Augusta needed on that Monday night!

During autumn football is very popular in the state, especially at the college level, and people were looking forward to seeing high school football games in the area on Friday night, the day of the storm. Rain would be a major inconvenience, to say the least! The storm had arrived earlier in the day, so games were rescheduled for the following Monday night. College football games that were scheduled for Saturday were also canceled due to the storm. So by Monday, after the major aspects of the storm had passed, many people looked forward to the rescheduled games being played that night. Ordinarily, Monday nights are reserved for professional football where at this time of year, *Monday Night Football* was airing on TV. So there would be a lot of football this Monday night, both on TV and in make-up high school games that were canceled on the previous Friday night because of the storm. But rain again threatened to cancel the area's high school games on this Monday night following the hurricane. But if that were to happen, there still would be the professional game on TV that fans could watch.

Strangely enough, it was Karen that liked watching football in the Tate household. Ted was more interested in soccer to go along with his commitments in business finance and investment. In addition to his job as security officer at the college, he owned a small but very profitable investment firm in Augusta. The boys were enrolled in middle school and were interested in music and other recreational activities.

So Karen really looked forward to an evening at home with the family and watching so professional football. She had also planned to prepare some pizza, and she makes a delicious homemade pizza. And everybody loves it!

Late that afternoon, Karen received a phone call from her local church that a call meeting had been scheduled for eight that evening. Obviously, Karen was not interested at all in going out on that Monday night because she really looked forward to being home with her family and watching a football game. Ted and the kids also looked forward to some of that good old homemade pizza that Karen had planned to make. But at the same time, Karen and Ted were dedicated members of their local church, and they tried to help out as much as possible in any way they could, depending on the issue at hand. The issue at hand was the kitchen and dining room renovation at the church. Karen believed that this project was not particularly urgent. That was because it dealt with something Karen thought could be taken care of at another time by hiring a contractor to meet with the congregation first and then schedule a time when he could come to make an evaluation of the kitchen and dining area of the sanctuary. After that, the contractor would lead, in Karen's view, the renovation efforts while informing the congregation of their progress.

In the end, Karen, being a dedicated church member, decided to attend the meeting. Ted would have gone, but he was busy doing some investment work. So Karen had hoped to leave home early enough to make the meeting then leave prior to its adjournment so she could return home, prepare the pizza, and look at most of the football game. She was likely to see at least the second half of the game, because it did not start until eight pm and usually was over by eleven. Karen thought that the pizza she had planned to make for Ted and the kids would possibly not get done! Oh well, if I end up not making the pizza hopefully they will understand; maybe they can make sandwiches instead, she reasoned. At any rate, she let everyone know her plans, and she began to prepare for going to her meeting.

The positive aspect to the whole issue facing Karen, however, was that she was providing service to the church. And for this, she got much enjoyment out of the prospect of her attending a meeting to offer her services if needed. But she did not anticipate getting involved in the details of the discussion they were to have that night. So after showering and getting dressed, off Karen went to her church call meeting!

When Karen left her house she did not anticipate having to negotiate a rainy night in Augusta. She didn't even bring an umbrella. But why should she? The day had been fair to clear, with only a small probability of rain for the evening, according to the local weather forecast. Besides, she thought that Hurricane Alex had dumped all the rain it had on the city over the weekend. In a small way, Karen was eager to get out of the house and wonder around the city because with the hurricane affecting the area all weekend, the family felt "trapped" in their home.

The church that Karen was going to was about thirty minutes from her home. In about ten minutes into her trip to the church, the rain started to fall at a fairly rapid pace! Then after a few minutes, the heavens seemed to open, so to speak, and it started to rain harder than she had ever known it to rain! At that point, Karen perceived a loud voice inside of her saying that she didn't have to go to the meeting and that it did not make any sense for her to continue, especially given the rain and the stormy conditions that were occurring. It was not an audible voice but rather a sense in her spirit that she should turn back! After all, Karen reasoned, and the loud voice inside her continued to confirm, Ted and the kids are very worried about her being out in these conditions. Karen could have called home to let them know that she was okay, but she had forgotten her cell phone!

Karen would later contend that it was very tempting to return to the comfort of her own home, on such a rainy evening as this, enjoying the comforts of being with husband and kids, and, not to mention, watching the football game! Karen was challenged in her spirit as the louder voice was catering to her flesh, her natural desire to return home and enjoy the evening with her family as opposed to a softer voice, the Holy Spirit, that encouraged her to keep her commitment and continue to her meeting (Mark 14:38).

It turned out not to be a difficult decision for Karen because she had a natural mentality to do what she thought was right regardless of anything that might pull her in another direction. So instead of giving in, so to speak, to that loud voice inside her that was a response to inclement weather conditions that night, she obeyed that gentle voice, the Holy Spirit, and continued to her church meeting (1 Peter 3:3, 4).

By the time Karen had arrived at the church, the rain had abated somewhat, and there were more cars in front of the church than she had expected, given the weather conditions that evening. *Thank goodness,* Karen thought! She had no umbrella to protect her from the rain! But fortunately, a little sprinkle in the air would not be to harmful to her, she thought. Besides, she had a roll of plastic in the backseat that she could use to avoid getting to wet.

Fortunately, Karen remembered that she had an extra umbrella in the trunk of her car, so she got it and walked a short distance to the church building and entered. She then came to the dining hall area in the basement of the sanctuary. This was where the meeting was being held. It was almost eight thirty, and the meeting had already started.

When Karen entered the meeting room, she found a good gathering of people, much more than she had expected. They were in the middle of a discussion on the business at hand, which was the renovation of the kitchen and dining areas. Karen usually offers her opinions in these kinds of meetings, but since she came in late after the proceedings had already started, she thought that she would reframe from active participation but rather would pay close attention to what was being said and offer any advice that may be asked of her. Soon the meeting would be over, she thought, and she could return home and see what probably would be the later stages of the football game. She believed that Ted and the kids probably would be in bed, she thought, and she could just relax, view the game, and quietly get ready for the next day.

However, things did not go according to these plans that Karen had that night. Little did she know that she would soon learn of some good news that would affect her work career! And it would come before the end of her church meeting. So just prior to the meeting being adjourned, the chair of the trustee board, who conducted the meeting, indicated that a visitor was present to give the people some important information about recent developments at Augusta State College, where Karen was a young professor. The visitor was a young lawyer named Attorney James.

Attorney James began his discussion by thanking the congregation present for allowing him to speak to them. He said he would be brief because he understood that everyone was eager to leave and return home. This certainly included Karen, anticipating her remaining evening hours in relaxation, looking at some football upon her return home. He brought good tidings to the gathering as he began to deliver his message. He indicated that the college was going through a transition period where it was mandated by the state college system that all instructors teaching at institutions of higher learning in the state were to obtain their terminal degrees within a reasonable period of time. The attorney indicated that the system's administrators needed to see that individuals employed at these institutions at least be in the process of working toward their degrees, either by finishing up their course work or completing a dissertation. In Karen's case, this meant that she needed to obtain the PhD degree in her area of biological sciences; she had already attained the master degree in that area of study. While Karen had been through a program at a terminal degree institution and had completed her course work, she had yet to start on writing a dissertation to be approved and subsequently become eligible to obtain the degree. More importantly, Karen was hired by the college with a stipulation that she would finish her degree requirements within a specified period of time. In short, she had not begun this process, so unless she could show evidence that she was in fact moving effectively toward completing the dissertation to obtain her degree, she would not be able to return to the college as an instructor in her department. It was just unclear when the school would decide to terminate a person like her because of insufficient progress toward attaining the degree.

Karen loved Augusta State when she first arrived on campus; she was treated fairly, she thought, by school officials when she was hired, and the cordiality of the school's administration, faculty, and students suggested a very good work environment. She thought then that she could remain in her position with only the masters for a very long time. Of course, she had to get positive evaluations from her peers as well as from students. But Karen was a very good teacher, and she worked well with her colleagues. Obviously, this was wishful thinking on the part of Karen, but little did she know, there would be a way out for her in her dilemma before the meeting adjourned.

Karen looked forward to resuming her work on completing her PhD requirements under the program talked about by Attorney James. This meant beginning to plan, write, and complete a dissertation in order to be eligible to obtain the degree. Karen now knew that her employment at the college was dependent upon her completing her degree requirements within a specified period of time.

So prior to the end of the meeting, Attorney James indicated what the college had to do to retain its standing as an academic institution of higher learning. He stressed that institutions would need to increase their percentage of faculty with terminal degrees to retain their academic standing. So Attorney James indicated that state administration would offer an official leave of absence to those who are already in a degree program and who could obtain the terminal degree by completing certain requirements. This leave of absence would include a year not being required to actively teach and perform other duties that may be required by the college while retaining full-time salary. It would be reserved exclusively for the faculty member completing the terminal degree.

Karen was very much interested in this opportunity. However, the challenge was that, in order to enter the program, Karen needed to complete a rather lengthy application process. It would have to be completed in one week by Monday of the following week, she thought. This would at least give her four working days to get her application completed! But who would she see at the college to get the process started? And what about all of the signatures and letters of support she would need to obtain? But she had to get it done somehow because she wanted to continue her work at Augusta State because she liked the environment there very much. It was an opportunity to finish her dissertation that she had not started to work on.

As Attorney James continued with the details of this program, he ended by saying that there was a deadline for completing the application by Friday morning at ten. "Friday morning" Karen cried! "That gives me even less time than I anticipated!" You see, because her church meeting was on Monday evening, she would have only Tuesday, Wednesday, and Thursday to complete the process. Only three days! So Karen had to see first of all, who had the application for her to complete the program and, secondly, what individuals and offices she needed to contact to complete it. Karen was positive, however, because she thought that she was a good candidate for the program. And besides, she had learned in Sunday school that for anything worth having, there is a cost, but God is there to help us in our time of need. So Karen proceeded on with a positive attitude and a lot of faith that everything would work itself out (Romans 8:28).

Eventually, when Attorney James finished his remarks, the church meeting finally came to a close. But before she left, Karen found that the attorney had with him the application materials that she so desperately needed to get the ball rolling, so to speak. "Thank the Lord!" Karen cried out. "At least one step is behind me. I can't wait to get home, look at a little football, and get a good night's rest so that I can put the effort into completing the application." Of course, this had to be done around her normal work schedule of teaching classes in the biology department.

When the meeting finally adjourned and Karen was on her way home, she found that the sky was in the process of clearing up, but there still was a little drizzle in the air. But you know what? Maybe her life was clearing up a little bit as well! The extra time spent at the meeting when the attorney delivered some valuable information to Karen and to others in attendance was a real blessing to her. But the blessing was a result of her obedience in listening to that soft voice within her, the Holy Spirit, encouraging her to continue to the meeting despite a rainy night in Georgia. She learned the next day that the attorney had left town after the church meeting. Had Karen not gone to the meeting that night, she may have never been made aware of the opportunity to obtain an official paid leave of absence from her duties at the college to complete her terminal degree that was necessary in her remaining at Augusta State.

She ended up returning home later than she expected, around ten thirty that night. The rain had abated by this time, and a rainy night in Georgia had finally come to an end, that is, until the next hurricane system would hit the state!

As she entered her house, she did find Ted and the kids in bed, with her only consolation at this point, after a long church meeting that she did not plan for, was the final few minutes of the football game that started at eight. By the way, the game involved the Atlanta Falcons playing the Green Bay Packers that evening. And Karen was thankful that she could at least, look at some of the game. This would be her only recreation that evening for Ted and the kids were fast asleep. However, she was even more thankful to God that she listened to the soft voice within her, encouraging her to attend the meeting. Thankfully, she did not obey the louder voice telling her to skip the meeting and return home.

By the way, Karen submitted her application on time and received her leave of absence from the college to work on her dissertation. She eventually completed it and went on to have a long, successful career at Augusta State College.

Watch and pray, lest you enter into temptation. The spirit is indeed willing but the flesh is weak.

—Mark 14:38

Do not let your adornment be merely outward-arranging the hair, wearing gold, or putting on fine apparel[4] *rather let it be the hidden person of the heart, with the incorruptible beauty of a gentle quiet spirit, which is very precious in the sight of God.*

—1 Peter 3:3–4

And we know that all things work together for good to those who love God, to those who are the called according to His purpose.

—Romans 8:28

GOD'S REALITY IN A SECULAR WORLD

9

The Garden

Trust in the Lord with all your heart,
and lean not on your own understanding.

—Proverbs 3:5

Rose Parker lives in Everett, Washington, which is a small suburban community just south of Seattle. Like most places in the Pacific Northwest region of the United States, there is a lot of rain and is cloudy throughout much of the year. The region around Seattle rests on the windward side of the Cascades, a mountainous region near the Pacific coast in the states of Washington and Oregon. Cool, moist air often blows in from the nearby Pacific Ocean and rises over the western slopes of the Cascades. The result is orographic precipitation that produces snow at the higher elevations and rain at the lower elevations; because of all the precipitation it seems like an almost endless period of cloudiness in the region that prevails. This description of the environmental setting in this part of the country is the reason for the growth of all types of vegetation, including the germination of plant seed in the soil, eventually producing the growth of all types of vegetable plants. So vegetable gardens are plentiful in the region.

Rose loves gardening. She is a single mom and lives with her son, Jackson, who is a sophomore at the local high school. Rose works as a realtor at a prominent real estate firm in Seattle. While she is a distributor for Mary Daye Productions in the Seattle area, the job she spends most of her time with is her realtor job, which allows for a great deal of independence. Therefore, she is able to spend any extra time she might have as an occasional speaker to civic clubs and other local organizations. She would mainly talk about the health of the real estate market in the Seattle region. She also hosts what are called "market parties" in her home where prospective buyers and renters come to listen to her lectures on opportunities to buy or rent houses in the region. On occasion she also markets commercial properties, but she says her focus is on discussing housing issues with families. Rose also teaches a Bible class to some members of her church on Tuesday evenings.

Rose does gardening as a hobby. She loves working in her vegetable garden in her rather large backyard. In addition to her garden, she grows all kinds of plants, including fruit trees, flowers, as well as the vegetables in her garden. There are all kinds of flowers, both seasonal and perennials. She is diligent about watering both her flowers and her vegetables but her heart is firmly set on taking care of her vegetable garden, as she refers to as affectionately as "the garden."

She finds that work in the garden in particular helps her state of mind, as well as contributing to some much-needed exercise, which she seldom gets on a regular basis because of her job. She often works long days at the office, and when she is not there she's on the road, speaking with groups or working with individual potential clients. Her son, Jackson, is a rather independent fellow, so she can simply leave him alone most of the time. Jackson is a very good student who plans to go to college and major in sports therapy. Although Jackson is a good kid, he does not help Rose much in the garden although he enjoys consuming the produce when it is harvested! Oh well.

So Rose's life constitutes a trilogy of Bible teaching, being a realtor, and having a garden. The sale of her Mary Daye products gets much less attention in her daily routine. But she loves to travel to the national conferences that promote the products and career opportunities in network marketing. Just last year, the convention was held in Las Vegas, and while dedicated to the conference, she found time to entertain herself and had lots of fun there. Some of Rose's church members frown on her visit to Vegas, sometimes called "Sin City." But fun in Vegas to Rose means enjoying herself without compromising her integrity. She even tried her hand at playing the slot machines but without much success. Her motto in life comes from the saying that do all things of value in moderation as led by the Spirit (1 Corinthians 6:12).

She loves connecting these activities together when she has the opportunity. For example, she often talks about how gardening is related to the biblical concept of sowing and reaping in her Bible study class. Also, each Thursday evening, when she hosts a weekly house party for potential clients, she would talk about her success as a gardener. The mix of Rose's faith and her job is quite interesting. The realtor business is known for helping people to find the right match between their personal desires for a residence and what is actually available for them in the local real estate market based on income. Rose's job is to help find that match.

Rose tries to make a connection between biblical principles and the personal needs, desires and interests of her students. It is an exciting adventure because people have different needs spiritually, and it is important to match that with what the Scripture says about those needs. And Rose knows that God is always with her, even in the secular real estate business. Rose realizes that while she is not an ordained minister, she has the responsibility to minister and teach when the opportunity arise (1 Timothy 4:10, 11). Despite her rather interesting life in real estate, however, Rose fines solace in the garden!

God's blessings are evident in many ways through the activity of gardening, and Rose utilized this to the fullest! Rose first tried her hand at gardening when she first moved to Everett. She would select an area in her back yard and till it with a rake and hoe in hand; the rather fertile soil was a product of the warm, moist weather conditions that prevailed in the region throughout the year. Planted seeds could easily be nurtured and would eventually grow and mature into useful, edible produce. Rose decided to make a rather large garden that would produce lots of vegetables at harvest time. Rose and Jackson loved to eat the vegetables that were picked from her garden, and Rose makes a great casserole from the spinach crop! So they typically had more than enough food, especially produce from the garden, for the long winter season that would come. And Jackson really looked forward to Rose making zucchini bread as a part of their meal at Christmas!

The challenging task that Rose confronted during the summer months was that after seed germination plants started to grow, and so did the weeds! They were competing for the same space as Roses' vegetable plants! Therefore

Rose had the task of keeping out as many of the weeds as she could, which became increasingly difficult as the growing season wore on during the long summer months. She had an opportunity to hire a horticulturalist to do the bulk of the work in her garden, but she felt that would take away the joy of working in the garden herself. She relished assisting the plants in their growth, treating them almost like children as they grew and matured to the point of their time to be harvested.

So in the first year, Rose continued with the maintenance of the garden, such as pulling weeds, spraying pesticides, and turning the soil. Furthermore, she anticipated harvesting crops when they matured. You might think that Jackson would help Rose in her work in the garden, but he wanted no part of it! He was much more interested in his school activities and future post-undergraduate studies.

One day in late August, it became apparent that the garden had become too difficult for Rose to manage effectively. There were weeds everywhere! Everywhere, that is, except the pathways between the rows of vegetable plants that she walked every day, caring for and managing her plants in the rows on both sides of a pathway. And she had created fourteen pathways between fifteen rows of vegetable plants. It was a large garden for one lady to manage! Anyway, the pathways she created because of her constant walking were weed-free, barren, and clear little elongated spaces or walkways between the rows of plants. A little spray of weed killer along the paths where she walked also helped to keep them clear. In these paths, she felt unimpeded in her attempt to pluck as many of the weeds from the row of vegetable plants as possible, as well as to harvest as much of the crop as she could at harvest time. With a clear path in between the plants, she also felt protected from harmful snakes, rodents, and other pests that might be hidden among the mass of weeds and plants that began to grow in each row as the season progressed.

One day Rose was in her kitchen preparing a good gourmet dish for guests she had invited to her market party, which was to take place later that afternoon. Rose stood in front of her kitchen window and, after placing a few utensils and dinner plates into the dishwasher, she noticed a large black line above the white sandy dirt that formed one of the clear paths where Rose could walk in her garden. As she stood there for what seemed to be for at least two minutes, mesmerized at what she was seeing out of the window, the line slowly disappeared. She immediately realized that what she just saw was a snake!

Judging from the length of time Rose just stood there gazing at the serpent, it seemed to have been several minutes. But actually, it was only a minute or two as she saw the snake slither across the path from her left to right and eventually disappeared into the adjacent weeded row where Rose's plants were growing. Rose was not very concerned about the situation, however, because she was accustomed to reptiles of all sorts, including snakes, when she worked as a vet assistant at the regional zoo in Seattle. In fact, unlike most people, Rose had an affinity for all reptiles; she would even handle, on occasion, some of the venomous snakes that were housed at the zoo. Notwithstanding any concerns of snakes being in her garden, she was not deterred from doing what she truly loved—caring for her vegetable plants!

Without giving it much thought about what she had just seen in her garden as she gazed out of her kitchen window, Rose continued to prepare for her guests that would be coming to her market party. After about thirty minutes, she returned to the sink in the kitchen, and, as she often did, viewed the amazing scenery outside her kitchen window. Rose would enjoy the simple things in nature; she would, for example, marvel at the ducks she would see swimming on the large lake beyond the fence in her backyard. They would often travel in groups of what seemed to be more than twenty in one single herd! Rose actually timed her work in the garden based on the time in which the herd of duck migrated from one end of the lake to the other, which was about ten every morning. Occasionally the ducks would wander on the street near where Rose lived, and one day she saw that one of them had been injured, but still barely alive, being hit by an inattentive motorist no doubt. It was lying helplessly on the side of the road. Being an animal lover, Rose stopped her car one day and gingerly took the animal to the local vet to be treated. She never got back with the vet to see if the creature survived, but she felt she did her part in satisfying the golden rule of treating others the way you would want to be treated. To Rose, it was more than just a duck!

During the growing season Rose would continue to appreciate what she had accomplished in the garden regardless of the challenges she had in keeping the weeds out. She was anxiously looking forward to telling her guests about her success as she would discuss mainly business related topics in the area of real estate financing. She might also throw in a biblical story or two for good measure!

Rose took advantage of the scenery beyond her backyard as she would often gaze out of her kitchen window when doing chores in that area of her home. She witnessed on this day unusually clear skies with much sunshine, with a scattering of patchy cumulus clouds as a celestial backdrop.

The blue sky and puffy white clouds provided a slightly moving reflection on the crystal blue waters in Lake Barrow. The water also reflected the snow-covered mountains in the background. *Oh my; what a sight!* she thought.

Then suddenly the majestic view outside of her kitchen window yield to an interesting dilemma for Rose. This was because she saw a large black line move across the pathway in her garden similar to what she had seen thirty minutes before in about the same location. "What is this?" Rose wondered to herself. Almost as quickly as this thought came to her mind, again, as before, the line slowly disappeared as she continued to gaze out of her window. This time, however, she perceived that the direction of the snakes' movement was in the opposite direction of what she had seen before; this time, the creature was slithering from right to left. Rose then shouted with a loud voice, with no one else around to hear her cries, "It's a snake!" She presumed that it was the same snake as she had seen before, making its way back across the path to the area in which it came.

As Rose thought about this occurrence, she began to wonder, What are the chances of seeing something like this happen? She pondered the question because she reasoned the chances of seeing this creature, in the same location, at two separate times about thirty minutes apart, is not very likely! So she concluded that it was more than simply a coincidence - that God was trying to reveal something to her. But what was He trying to reveal? Rose thought. "What does this mean?"

In Bible study, she realized that the Holy Spirit is present in all believers to help us in a time of need. But in this situation, there was no apparent immediate need. Rather, she sensed that God was trying to tell her something through this experience. Was God speaking to her in some way, perhaps, to warn her of the dangers of her continuing to work in the garden? At this point it was not clear to her about the meaning of what she had just experienced. Rose eventually realized that God, through the Holy Spirit, was trying to tell her something that would be of benefit to her in the future.

As Rose continued to ponder the experience, she felt that seeing the serpent at the same location at separate times was more than a chance occurrence. She reasoned that the Spirit was apparently speaking to her. The question was the meaning of this occurrence. Rose finally concluded that God, through the Holy Spirit, was trying to reveal to her the dangers of constantly working in the garden, not knowing if she would accidently come into contact with a venomous serpent. While in the natural, she would not be able to detect a potential danger, having her hand unprotected, plucking weeds from her vegetable garden. But she realized that God, being all-knowing, would know the dangers of her continuing to work in the garden. So at this point, it was *decision time*! Should Rose disregard what she thought to be God speaking to her through the Holy Spirit and continue to work in the garden? Or should she heed what she believed God was providing to her—His favor in giving her revelation about a potentially dangerous situation?

So Rose did make the decision, and it was to heed what she believed that God was trying to reveal to her and eliminate her work in the garden that she loved so much. But Rose would later make another decision, that being to keep her garden but hire a horticulturalist to manage it. In the end, Rose used godly wisdom to keep what she really wanted, the garden, without compromising what she believed God was trying to reveal to her. So she continued to have the garden she loved so much but without her having the responsibility to manage it.

But Rose continued her work in a rather large backyard, attending to other plants outside of her vegetable garden that would not present a threat because of an overabundance of weed growth; such was the case in her garden. Also, Rose would eventually join an athletic club where she could exercise on a regular basis and, in a way, fill the void left by her absence from working in the garden.

With a drastic change in her daily activity pattern, Rose continued to enjoy the view from her kitchen window of her backyard with all of its plants, including her vegetable garden, as well as the lake with its duck crossings and the majestic mountains in the background.

There are enumerable instances where God may bless us without our knowledge. How many accidents and misfortunes have we avoided by following the guide of the Holy Spirit? Did your car not start on a cold winter morning for example? Only God knew that maybe you avoided being in an accident by not driving to work that day. Or have you ever missed an opportunity to purchase a house that you really wanted? Perhaps God knew of a better house in a nicer neighborhood. Or did you miss a plane flight to a critical business meeting you were scheduled to attend? Perhaps you missed a flight that would not make it to its destination.

Rose may never know what negative outcome she may have avoided as a result of her acknowledging what she perceived as the Holy Spirit speaking to her and therefore making a decision to not to work in the garden again. But this is when our trust in God kicks in, in times when we don't fully understand some life's experiences and what the Holy Spirit may be saying to us through those experiences (Proverbs 3:5-6). In our faith walk, we have to trust that God is doing what is best for us whether the blessing manifests itself or not.

> *All things are lawful for me, but all things are not helpful. All things are lawful for me, but I will not be brought under the power of any.*
>
> —1 Corinthians 6:12

> *For to this end we both labor and suffer reproach, because we trust in the living God, who is the Savior of all men, especially of those who believe.* [11]*These things command and teach.*
>
> —1 Timothy 4:10–11

> *Trust in the Lord with all your heart, and lean not on your own understanding.* [6]*In all your ways acknowledge Him, And He shall direct your paths.*
>
> —Proverbs 3:5-6

ALL THINGS WORK TOGETHER FOR GOOD

10

Bad Neighborhood

And we know that all things work together for good to those who love God, to those who are the called according to His purpose.

—Romans 8:28

Bill Rawls has a very close family with strong moral values. Bill works as the local manager of a large global trucking firm based in Phoenix, Arizona. His wife Anna is a child care provider in the city of Flagstaff, a suburb just beyond the city limit of Phoenix. They have three children, a son Jay and two daughters, Monica and Joda. Everyone is very busy during the week, including the kids where Jay is on the track team at school and has an active hobby in doing art work. The two girls are avid sports fans, especially Monica, who is a standout on her middle school basketball team. Her parents and siblings are proud fans cheering for her and the home team at basketball games! And Joda, the youngest of the bunch, well, she's just Joda; what a personality! And oh yea, she plays basketball too!

To relax after a long week of activity, the Rawlses often travel to the nearby mountains where they love to hike and camp out. When the family is not on the road during the weekends, they usually attend church on Sunday at the Spring View Christian Church in Phoenix. All are active members where her husband Bill, leads the way as a church administrator.

Proximity to Bill's job was a strong reason for the Rawlses' decision to move to Scottsdale, a bit further away from Flagstaff where Anna works and from Phoenix where the kids are in school. But Bill wanted to move to Caleb County, and for one reason that being that it would be a nice, safe neighborhood! Bill had read earlier about how nice some of the neighborhoods were in that part of the metropolitan area. Many of these counties were designated as having some of the highest incomes in the country. He felt that the family could afford the move because of his recent hiring as a manager at Dennings Distribution, a global company that distributes farm equipment to local retailers. While the salary that was offered to Bill was rather modest, the opportunity for upward advancement in the company was very good. Some of the key personnel in the company had reminded him of such during the hiring process. So after Bill and Anna had researched the various homes in the Scottsdale area, and in particular a neighborhood that they felt comfortable in establishing a residence, they decided on a house in Chandler's Heights.

The house that Bill and Anna finally considered was a nice one in Chandler's Heights. But before they were to make a final decision, Bill wanted to research the community in which the house was located. The character of neighborhood and community was also important to the Rawlses in their decision to purchase the house. Bill and his family debated whether to finalize on this particular house or continue their search. Bill took the extra time because he wanted to be comfortable with the neighborhood surrounding the house as well.

To make sure that the neighborhood was a good one to move into, Bill would drive around the community after work, especially in the early evening, to see if there was a lot of foot traffic in the area, as well as to check the noise level. He also wanted to see if pets were running around, like dogs and other stray animals. After driving through the neighborhood on two or three occasions, he saw nothing that would discourage him from moving into the area. In fact, he found that the neighborhood was a rather quiet and peaceful community.

It was a week after Bill drove around in the neighborhood when the decision on moving to Chandler's Heights had been confirmed. So with all the information on both the house and the surrounding neighborhood that they thought they needed, the Rawlses closed on the property and started what they hoped would be several peaceful years enjoying their new home. They looked forward to raising their kids in a nurturing environment as they continued in middle school and later in high school.

Chandler's Heights was a very attractive neighborhood with mostly two-story homes with fenced-in backyards. The homeowners association made sure that the lawns were mowed on a regular basis and that plants were kept trimmed. In addition, most yards were well manicured and edged. As an extra benefit, there was a swimming pool, lounge area, and exercise facilities in the community clubhouse! And most important to Bill, it was quiet at night.

Weekdays were quiet times for the Rawlses after work for the first several weeks of living in the Chandler's Heights neighborhood. On most weeks, the Rawlses would attend

Bible study, and by the end of the week, the kids would go to choir rehearsal. So the Rawlses were dedicated to the church, but more importantly, lead by Bill, they believed that the biblical principle that we show the love of Christ by being obedient to His Word, which means loving our neighbor and being of service to others. So the Rawlses did a lot of community service, including assisting in a community-based meals-on-wheels program, participation in a prison ministry, and visits to the local nursing home. On Sundays, the family would attend church in the late morning and early afternoon and were usually back home by two.

One of the reasons for the Rawlses decision to move to Scottsdale, some fifty miles away from Phoenix where Bill worked, was the problem of violence in some of the city's neighborhoods, especially in the southern part of the city, which included a community called Claremont. Some of these areas such as Claremont were notorious for illegal gambling, prostitution, and street violence. One of the characteristics of this part of the city was that most of the issues of criminal activity were time specific, so to speak. That is, most of the overt criminal activity usually took place at night, especially late night and during the early morning hours. As a result, public safety issues were a concern for local law enforcement officials to address this problem. Police substations were strategically placed in communities like Claremont to at least limit or preferably eliminate entirely criminal activity in the area. This idealistic vision of a crime free area was not realistic, but still the police wanted to limit criminal activity in the area by noticeable surveillance.

Over a period of time, after the first few years of the Rawlses' residence in their new neighborhood, Bill was able to take a two-week break from his work, sort of like a vacation. He was at home during that period during the daytime hours when most adults in the neighborhood were at work and children in school. Bill had taken these breaks from work before, and he found the neighborhood to be very quiet during this time of day. During his latest time off from work, when he went to his house early, he began to detect a different situation in the area. He began to notice that a few gradual changes were taking place in the neighborhood. First, he noticed that the number of renters in the area had grown since they first moved to the neighborhood. Second, graffiti was beginning to appear in certain places, like fences, some of the sidewalks, and on vacant houses. Third, and most importantly, there seemed to be more activity in the streets of the neighborhood than before, especially in the early afternoon period of the day. When Bill returned to work, and the days continued into weeks, there seemed to be, in Bill's estimation, less and less quietness in the neighborhood than during their first few years living in the area.

Eventually, things got to be noticeably worse during the daytime. Evidence of this was when, on one afternoon, Anna returned home from her day care job because she was not feeling well. As she approached the entrance to the main gate of her neighborhood, she noticed some young men. They seemed to be teenagers sitting on a bench not very far from her house. She thought that it was odd that they were there instead of being in school. Anyway, she continued to drive up to her house and proceeded to get out of her car. She had done this on several occasions before but not necessarily at that time of day because of her work at the day care.

As she walked to her front door, one of the young boys approached her and asked if she needed any help with the shopping bags that she had. She had just been to the grocery store and had planned to make some hotdogs that night. Anna was startled that anyone would come that close to her when no one else could be seen in the area except for the boy who approached her and his friends. It was rather unnerving! She quickly responded that she was fine and thanked him for his assistance. The young man returned to his small group that was only a short distance away. Meanwhile, Anna had just been scared out of her boots! The boys clearly did not appear to be a friendly group as perceived by Anna. One of the young men was smoking a cigarette, and another boy looked to be drinking something out of a cup. Anna wondered it could be some alcoholic beverage. And they were constantly gazing at Anna as she entered her house.

When Anna was safely into her home, she locked the doors and got on the phone to call Bill to inform him of the experience. She said that she felt very uncomfortable with the boys hanging out so close to their house, just hanging out with no apparent objective. They were just there and on occasion would gaze at their house. Bill said he would come home early to survey the situation and to comfort Anna from what she had just experienced. So Bill left work and arrived at his neighborhood a short time later. He saw the young boys near his house as Anna had seen! Bill went into his house and remained at home for the rest of the day. While finally at home, he comforted Anna and enjoyed a rare opportunity to rest at home during a weekday. And by the way, he enjoyed some good hotdogs and baked beans that night.

Bill decided to research what he considered to be a changing neighborhood. On one occasion, he visited the local library and read books and reviewed documents on population issues that pertained to the local area. What he found was very interesting! Criminal activity in the area had grown by over 50 percent. He was very thorough in his research, which included a review of census documents summarizing population changes in the area. Interestingly enough, most of the criminal activity occurred in the metropolitan Phoenix area, particularly in the central city, between nine pm and five am. Moreover, he read that the presence of illegal activity in the city was, according to police records, tied to the much of the violence that the city had experienced over the past two years.

More disturbing to Bill and his family was that he found that nationally people involved in organized street crime within the central city had moved their residence from the central cities to the suburban areas, like Scottsdale. But the purpose of this move was not to carry on the devious activities in a new location. The real purpose was apparently to move their residence from an area where they were suspected of being involved in criminal activity to a non-suspecting residential area where there was little or no police presence as they were concentrated in the central cities. Therefore Bill reasoned that many gang members were likely living in neighborhoods like Chandler's Heights and could be seen on occasion in the early afternoon.

About three weeks from the time Anna had first seen the young men on the street near her house, she again came home in the early afternoon. As before, she saw young men near her house! She was disturbed this time as before. Again, she called Bill, who came home immediately to monitor the situation. When Bill got to his house, he confronted the fellows and had some words with them about congregating near his house. Nothing came of that confrontation, however.

When Bill came into the house and met with Anna, she tearfully admitted that she was terrified of what could happen in the neighborhood and to her as well as to the kids. It was evident that this type of environment was not a favorable one for them and, especially for the children. So Bill became increasingly concerned of the situation. He especially thought of Anna being at home alone in an environment that was increasingly more unstable with regards to the kind of people that were beginning to infiltrate and take residence the neighborhood. You see, among the duties that Bill had on his job at Dennings was sometimes taking long trips to other cities around the the US, as well as cities in other countries on occasion, to attend meetings and to conduct workshops. So his concern grew for Anna and the kids being in such a changing and possibly hostile environment whenever he was away from the house for several days.

At this point, Bill started to make plans to move out of the neighborhood and into some other area in the Phoenix metro area. The challenge Bill and his family had was finding a buyer for his current home while, at the same time, finding a suitable residence elsewhere and close on that property. Still, the family would be at the current house at least for the near future, and Bill knew that the longer they remain there, the more risky that some confrontation would take place between him and whomever might present some challenge, like those young men that congregated near his house.

The situation had gotten to the point where Bill sought spiritual council on the matter from his pastor, Reverend Lendon. So about two weeks after Bill had the confrontation with the young boys near his house, he decided to call his pastor concerning those issues. So on a Thursday evening Bill gathered the family together and made a call to the pastor. The pastor prayed with Bill and his family for their safety as well as for their comfort in living peacefully in the neighborhood. The family certainly needed that because of the circumstances that they found themselves in. Such a situation could have easily resulted in heightened stress levels for the whole family, and it started to affect Anna in a negative way. But Bill noticed that after the prayer with his pastor that there was such a release in his spirit; he felt that a weight had been taken from on top of him! He was as light as a feather! From that point on, he felt more confident that God would intervene and remedy the situation in some way although he was unsure how things would eventually turn out.

What happened over the next two weeks was truly remarkable. After intensive house searches by Bill and Anna, they concluded that a house in Flagstaff, almost on the Phoenix city limit, would make the most sense to them as a permanent residence. Like what they did in Chandler's Heights, Bill did his research on the house as well as the neighborhood and felt very good about the area in general. It was closer to the central city than his residence in Chandler's Heights, where one would think that criminal behavior would be more frequent. However, Bill found that this area was the one the family ended up strongly considering to be their next home, and it appeared to be a very good neighborhood. It would be a scaled-down version of the house they had before, but the area was very quiet.

So they were ready to close, but they still had to sell their house in Chandler's Heights because they were going to use some of the funds from the sale of that home as a down payment on the new house. Fortunately, the very day the Rawlses were to move into their new residence, they received a call from the realtor they had been working with. The realtor said to Bill that an individual had made an offer to buy their old house! And they were willing to move in immediately! "Praise the Lord!" Bill proclaimed. There was a lot of movement and transactions taking place on that day of the move. So the Rawlses ended up concluding on the bid for the sale of their old home and, at the same time, closing on their new residence. There was a lot of activity going on that day for the Rawlses, but it was well worth the trouble!

In the instance of Bill's family having a home in what had become a bad neighborhood, things ultimately worked out perfectly for them (Romans 8:28). Certainly, in the Rawlses case, God's favor was with them!

> *And we know that all things work together for good to those who love God, to those who are the called according to His purpose.*
>
> —Romans 8:28

HALTING BETWEEN TWO DECISIONS

11

The Spirit of Nonaction

Do not say "I will recompense evil":
wait for the Lord, and He will save you.

—Proverbs 20:22

Jefferson High School is unique. Unlike most high schools, Jefferson developed its academic program into four units of instruction. They are science and mathematics,arts, business, and social sciences. The school is constantly placed on an exclusive list as one of the top prep institutions in the country, with over 90 percent of its students attending college. Jim Meyer was employed as a geology teacher in the science and mathematics unit at the school.

Jim is single and lives in an upscale neighborhood in Burnsville, Minnesota, a suburb south of Minneapolis. One of the things Jim loves about Jefferson High is its quality academic program. His first choice of employment was always Southern Wisconsin University in the school of environmental studies. Jim was a recent graduate of the University of Minnesota in the ecological studies department where he attained honors in his area of study, which was historical geology with a focus on the study of dinosaurs.

After a brief job search process, Jim found that a teaching position was available in his specialty area at Southern. Wow! How fortunate! So he applied for the position but was confronted with stiff competition for the job he really coveted. While he was a finalist for a permanent position in geology at this school, Jim lost out to a more experienced individual that had a much stronger record in formal research. "Well, better fortune next time," Jim lamented. Soon after that experience, a position in the same discipline that Jim had been trained became available at another school. But it was not a college or university, it was a high school! It was Jefferson High in south Burnsville, only a short distance from where Jim lived. Jim had a deep respect for what high schools provided, preparing young people for life in the world of work or continuing with their education. But Jim had his sights set on teaching at the college level, not in high school. Nonetheless, the position at Jefferson seemed to be acceptable because of the school's strong academic standing. So Jim ended up teaching at Jefferson for most of his career, which was almost twenty-five years.

One of the most popular courses in the geology curriculum at Jefferson High was the study of dinosaurs, which Jim taught from the very beginning of his tenure at the school. It is a unique course of study in a high school curriculum. How many high schools have a course on dinosaurs? Well, Jefferson does! Jefferson is more than a typical high school; it is among a selected few preparatory institutions in the country that focus on helping gifted students enter some of the best colleges and universities. And Jefferson was the only high school that Jim knew of that had a course on this subject although no one taught it prior to his arrival. This boded well with Jim, who had trained in this subject and ended up teaching it at Jefferson.

The course on dinosaurs was a popular one. And while enrollment in the course was relatively small in comparison to most of the other courses, a case could be made that it is the most popular course at the school. You see, many of the other courses are required where students must enroll in and complete them in order to graduate. Students are automatically steered toward them. However, the study of dinosaurs course is different. It is an elective where students enroll not because they are required to take it but rather because they want to take it. It's just that popular. Of course, Jim has a lot to do with that because he is a good teacher. But then again, there are many good teachers at Jefferson who don't attract the students that Jim does! So why is Jim's course more popular than the others, and why are students more easily attracted to his course? The answer lies in the school's theatrical studio, which is located in the arts unit.

The theatrical studio is where plays are presented and movies are shown. The plays were produced on the campus and using members of the student body as the actors in the various productions. In fact, the studio has gain national recognition and has attracted movie producers and other agents from Hollywood in California. Knowing the quality of the technology Jefferson has in this area, as well as the dedicated faculty, staff, and administration, the movie industry had considered Jefferson as a model of onsite production of movies and plays and where students could receive top-notched training in the arts and in the technology of the movie industry. Among the credits that the unit has received in this regard include productions on the *Planet of the Apes* movie series. And some of the students in the program have visited Hollywood as interns to learn more about the moviemaking business. At any rate, Jim had benefited enormously from this unique connection between his unit of science and mathematics and the arts unit.

While Jefferson High had been a model of stability for decades, recently there have been challenges that the institution had not experienced before. At the forefront of important issues confronting the school was the reorganization of its academic structure. The unit structure had received an increased number of attacks, primarily from the state legislature, concerning the increased cost of running the program. The arts unit in particular had been targeted because of the high operational costs in that area. So providing an education to high school students in the arts became threatened. In short, the central administration, an area of state government in charge of providing funding necessary to sustain high school programs, deemed that the unit structure for the curriculum at Jefferson High was too costly to be sustained. What was recommended was a replacement to this system with a new focus on individual departments. The central administration estimated that thousands of dollars could be saved per year by eliminating the unit structure at Jefferson.

Despite Jefferson's high level of stability over most of its history, challenges were coming not only from outside of the campus from state administration but also from within. Challenges from within the school were manifested over the past year as Jefferson experienced a significant turnover particularly in school administration. Specific changes in Jim's unit in particular would present career changes for him. So while his remaining on the faculty at the school was not in jeopardy, the volume and quality of materials used in his unit might be severely compromised.

The most important change in the science and mathematics unit that would affect Jim was the resignation of the unit's director and longtime friend Arthur Bryant. Arthur had known Jim for some time. In fact, Arthur was instrumental in getting Jim hired at the school. You see, Arthur had joined Jefferson after retiring as head of the ecological studies department at Southern Wisconsin University where geology was being taught. Of course, this was the same department that Jim had applied to after finishing graduate school. In fact, Arthur was the chairman of the committee that rejected Jim's application in favor of a more experienced professor. Arthur was in favor of selecting Jim for the job, but most of his colleagues on the committee voted for a more experienced candidate. They were more concerned about keeping a stable department with a more experienced professor than with taking the risk of hiring a young, untested recent graduate such as Jim. Arthur also was extremely concerned about keeping a stable department, but the difference between him and his colleagues was that he believed that hiring a young, albeit untested, recent graduate, such as Jim, would allow the department to retain its stability while taking advantage of Jim's qualities in formal research, a quality that the other candidates did not have. In the end, while Arthur did vote for Jim coming on board, there were not enough votes for Jim to be selected. However, there was some consolation. You see, because of Arthur's connections to Jefferson extend way back when he was in graduate school, he was instrumental in getting Jim hired there.

While Jim was beginning his teaching career at Jefferson, Arthur worked a few more years at Southern before retiring. When Arthur finally retired from Southern years later, he continued to have a desire to be an administrator at a smaller institution.

Soon after his retirement from Southern, Arthur moved on and did something much different than what he had done before as an administrator. He accepted an opportunity to again be an administrator, this time at a high school, Jefferson High. Well, how about that? Arthur was reunited with Jim and still not ready to totally retire from what he loved to do, which was being able to affect the lives of young people, so he became the head of the science and mathematics unit at Jefferson. It was a natural transition for Arthur to move from his administrative position at Southern to a similar position at Jefferson High. Besides, the position as unit head had just become available because of the unexpected departure of its previous head. At any rate, Arthur ended up being Jim's superior for several years as head of the science and mathematics unit at Jefferson, and they worked closely together. Arthur was well liked not only by Jim but by other members of the science faculty, and Jim's program in particular continued to grow in prestige.

Eventually, however, it was decided that Arthur should be released from his position as head of the science and mathematics unit at Jefferson. This action was a reflection of the changes taking place in Jefferson's curriculum structure by central administration. This action was a tremendous disappointment to Jim as well as to the unit as a whole. But it was the manner in which the changes took place that affected Jim the most—changes that would affect not only Arthur, but the program Jim directed that had grown so much.

So as a part of the many changes taking place at Jefferson, Arthur was replaced by Dr. Carolyn Sally as head of the science and mathematics unit. Dr. Sally was attracted to Jefferson's administration because it felt that she could lead the school more in the direction of formal research and in the procurement of federal grants. An additional feather in her cap was that she had been employed for a while at the federal science foundation where she was the director of grants and contracts for colleges and universities. Well, Dr. Sally had planned to use the same skills she had at the foundation at Jefferson High. This was a big plus for the school, especially in the climate of decreasing financial assistance from the state government. This was a similar situation Arthur found himself in at his old school, Southern Wisconsin, involving Jim, who was applying for a position there but was dismissed in favor of a more experienced administrator. This time, again, it looked like it would not work out in Jim's favor because his friend Arthur had been replaced.

Sure enough, Arthur's replacement, Dr. Sally, was a younger administrator who had more experience in research and grants than he did. What would Jim do now without Arthur being around as head of the unit? His friend and supervisor had been replaced with someone else! It certainly was something that Jim had to get accustomed to, not having his friend Arthur around. While the geology program under Jim's direction grew significantly for the first several years after his hiring at Jefferson prior to Arthur's arrival, it grew at an even faster rate after Arthur came on board. So as Arthur had been released from his position, Jim said to himself, "I'll just have to adjust to a new supervisor."

Little did Jim know that his new unit head would bring drastic changes to the school that would affect his career! Dr. Sally really wanted to give herself another challenge in her work career. So she apparently saw an opportunity to enhance an already effectively administered preparatory high school into becoming an even more dynamic academic institution at the high school level. She especially was interested in continuing the school's tradition of preparing its students for college. Dr. Sally was motivated to enhance an existing excellent academic program at Jefferson and, as a result, wanted to put her own stamp on the school's academic structure. Therefore she moved quickly to reorganize the unit structure at Jefferson! She did this with the blessings of the school's head administration overseeing all four units on the campus.

After a few weeks of review of Jefferson's curriculum, Dr. Sally and selected head administrators at the school decided that the separate units at Jefferson should not only be seriously evaluated but that the structure itself should be changed as soon as possible! Besides, Dr. Sally thought, the central administration would like to see positive, cost saving measures in the school's academic structure, even if it meant affecting her position in that structure as well.

After several meetings with key administrators had taken place, decisions for reorganization were made. One of the decisions relating to this reorganization was the transfer of Jim's department, geology, from the science and mathematics unit to the arts unit. However, these decisions were made without the knowledge of Jim's department chairperson, Dr. Mason, who worked directly under the unit of science and mathematics head, Dr. Sally. Dr. Mason had not been made aware of all the oncoming changes at the school and certainly not aware that one of his prized faculty members, Jim Meyer, would soon be moved to another unit. This change would not only affect the science department but could also affect Jim and his tenure at the school, which it did! Eventually, Jim did get the information about the reorganization that would ultimately affect him and his career at Jefferson, but his department chair remained uninformed about the changes that were to come.

Jim got the information on the fate of the geology program, located in the science department of the science and mathematics unit, at the end of a work day. Jim was clearing his desk from a busy day of teaching. He had just finished looking through some of the mail delivered that day. One of the items he received was a letter from Dr. Sally. In the letter she began by saying how valuable he was to the success of the school. She continued to say that it had been decided that the geology program in the unit of science and mathematics was been transferred to the unit of arts. In this unit, it would be an independent program; so he would not be associated with a particular department. She stated further that he had only three weeks to empty his office and relocate to that unit on the campus. Fortunately, the unit of arts was located only a short distance away from where Jim had been housed for several years in the unit of science and mathematics.

Jim anticipated that the relocation would end up being a straightforward, noneventful process, only a little inconvenient. But after really thinking about the situation, it would be not a little inconvenient—it would be very a time-consuming, energy-sapping adventure into a new situation on the campus! Jim had to transport all his materials that he had accumulated over the years from one unit to another! So what Jim thought at first would be a fairly simple process turned out to be more difficult.

In addition to the challenge of the physical move, Jim would also have to get accustomed to seeing his colleagues in the science and mathematics unit less frequently. He had befriended many of them over the years. The natural tendency was for Jim to be offended at Dr. Sally's actions because she had not discussed the move with him, nor had it been discussed with his department chair, Dr. Mason.

Jim attended his last department meeting where he informed the chair about the letter he received from Dr. Sally. At the beginning of the meeting, Jim told his colleagues who were present of his removal from the science department. Of course, everyone was very surprised and dismayed at the news. That is when the chair, Dr. Mason, indicated that he had not been notified of Dr. Sally's actions and, like the rest of the faculty, was shock at what had transpired. Jim was especially surprised that even his immediate supervisor, Dr. Mason, had not been notified. "Oh my!" Jim gasped. Not only that, but all his colleagues, who were very loyal to Jim and his program, could not believe it! At any rate, Dr. Mason felt that the science and mathematics unit and especially his department would be hurt very much by Jim's departure because of his friendly demeanor as well as his professional contribution to the department, especially as it relates to his course in the study of dinosaurs.

Jim had a very vocal personality and often spoke his mind on various school issues. At the same time, he usually did not rush into empty dialogue about someone whom he may consider to be unfair to him. So while Jim did not totally understand the actions of Dr. Sally of not communicating such important information to the people most affected by her actions, he was not bitter toward her. He basically accepted the decision made by Dr. Sally and prepared for the move. He passed the whole episode off as simply a difference between Dr. Sally and himself regarding to methods of handling changes in the curriculum. But he realized that he was not an administrator, only a faculty member working at the behest of his superior, Dr. Sally. She was in charge, so Jim relented to the decisions made by her. So Jim dutifully packed his belongings and, within a week, had moved the short distance to his new office, and to his new unit, the arts unit.

While not overly religious, Jim had a very strong moral tempest that guided his actions. So Jim could have asked God why this move happen? Things were just fine where Jim had been for the past twenty-five years, especially with Arthur coming over to be head in his unit of science and mathematics. But Jim decided not to voice his concern to Dr. Sally and to indicate his displeasure about the lack of discretion that he felt was displayed by the new unit head.

Given his knowledge of the discipline of geology, the structure of the science and mathematics unit, as well as the unit structure concept at the school, Jim probably could have taken action and possibly succeeded in confronting Dr. Sally. After all, she had limited knowledge of the units on campus and her decision to make such a drastic, curriculum change did not sit well either with Jim or his colleagues. So Jim, being well respected among his peers, could have possibly encouraged Dr. Sally to reverse her decision. But Jim was a complete team player and was known to not voice his concerns about decisions made by his superiors unless there was ample evidence to support his view. He simply was at peace in situations that were anything but peaceful (John 14:27)!

While unrest and instability in the curriculum was happening all around at Jefferson, Jim assumed that his superiors were doing what was in the best interest of the school, including Dr. Sally's actions. Jim's non-action or non-response to the decision to move his program to another unit was an opportunity for him to trust God that He would ultimately be delivered to a better situation because of the experience (Psalm 91:15). This trust was based on Jim's remembering how God was with him in situations in the past when he always came out of the experience in a better position than before. That's what happened when he was not selected for a position at Southern Wisconsin University that he had applied for years earlier, a position he really wanted. That rejection, certainly a negative situation that Jim felt at the time, did not get any better when the only position available after this experience was in a high school, Jefferson High. But his desire was to not work at a high school. Since Jim always had a vision of teaching at the college level upon obtaining his graduate degree, he was very disappointed, although thankful, for becoming employed at Jefferson.

Despite Jim's disappointment of not being hired where he really wanted to be, he laid claim to perhaps the most amazing scripture in the Bible, Romans 8:28, "All things work together for good to those who love God, to those who are the called according to His purpose."

What a remarkable scripture! Whatever we're going through or negative experience we have in our life, if we "love God and are the called according to His purpose," it is guaranteed from the Scripture that we will ultimately benefit from any negative experience we might have. Seems almost unbelievable and virtually impossible based on some of the circumstances that we sometimes find ourselves. Consider these scenarios: the death of a love one, the end of a romantic relationship, a divorce, the loss of a job, a major health problem. Sometimes it is difficult to see how some of the things we are confronted with can benefit us. But as believers, we quickly realize that "with God, all things are possible" (Matthew 19:26). Moreover, the Scripture assures us that whatever problems we're going through or issues we may have, they will work together for our good if we love God and are called into His plans.

So in the natural, Jim thought how his situation with Dr. Sally could turn out for his good. "Can't see it," he moaned. But Jim had a tendency to "go with the flow," so to speak. Jim's decision not to act or respond in the matter provided no resistance to Dr. Sally's decision and therefore guaranteed that the move would in fact be made. Also, with his moral tempest in place, Jim saw this circumstance as an opportunity to do a good deed, to give the new administrator the benefit of the doubt, so to speak, as she adapted to her new administrative position (Galatians 6:10). Jim simply figured that God would arrange things so that he would be better off than before as a result of the change. And you know what? That's exactly what happened!

Because of his transfer to the arts unit he made communication with officials from Hollywood much more often now than when he was in the science and mathematics unit. As a result, his program was more visible than ever. He would not have experienced this benefit had it not been for his rejection at Southern Wisconsin; if that were to have happened, he would not have ended up at Jefferson and his whole career would have been altered. Also, Jim's decision not to resist the change in the curriculum that would affect his program, as a result of Dr. Sally's actions, proved to be very beneficial. You see, Jim's program, which included the course, the study of dinosaurs, now had the opportunity to work directly with the faculty in the arts unit who benefited from his course materials because they were far more accessible to be utilized. In addition to these benefits, Jim's relocation to the arts unit resulted in a salary increase by some 20 percent over what he received in his former unit. So the geology program functioned very well within his new unit, the arts.

The lesson of this story is that the Holy Spirit residing in us does not always lead us into action, such as in response to a real or a perceived wrongful action or injustice toward us. To the contrary, sometimes we are led to simply wait and trust that God will work things out on our behalf. In such cases, as with Jim Meyer, the best action to take is really to utilize a spirit of nonaction—a trust in God that He will take action on our behalf. But for God to work most effectively for us, it requires our willingness to lean on Him when we are led to do so by the Holy Spirit. This response by Jim turned out to be the best thing that could have happened to him in his professional career.

> *Peace I leave with you, my peace I give to you; not as the world gives do I give to you. Let not your heart be troubled neither let it be afraid.*
>
> —John 14:27

He shall call upon Me, and I will answer him; I will be with him in trouble; I will deliver him and honor him.

—Psalm 91:15

But Jesus looked at them and said to them, "With men this is impossible, but with God all things are possible."

—Matthew 19:26

Therefore, as we have opportunity, let us do good to all, especially to those who are of the household of faith.

—Galatians 6:10

MY GOD IS AWESOME!

12

Perfect Timing

Be strong and of good courage, do not fear nor be afraid of them: for the Lord your God, He is the One who goes with you. He will not leave you nor forsake you.

—Deuteronomy 31:6

Janine always had an adventurous spirit; she would not take no for an answer if she really believed in something. In high school she always wanted to pursue a career in engineering. But being from Petersburg, a small town in the southern part of Virginia, she felt that earning a degree in this area was not possible at the local university, which was named Edenton U, because of its curriculum. Janine's parents were excited because as a student in high school, she could get a scholarship to attend Edenton U. This would benefit her parents as college expenses would be paid and they thought she would get an excellent education at Edenton.

Since Edenton U did not have the specialty areas that would help Janine pursue her career goals, she decided that she wanted to go to college away from home, to a school that did have the specialty area she desired. For weeks, there was a tug-of-war, so to speak, between Janine and her parents. Janine eventually got her way and ended up attending a larger school, P & P University, which was located in

Chester, Virginia, a four hour drive from Petersburg. Janine was content at this school because it had a curriculum that included the courses she needed to take to get a degree in civil engineering. P & P had an established degree program in this subject area, so Janine was very confident that she could get the education she needed there to realize her career dreams as a civil engineer. She was looking forward to reaching her career goals and she was away from home!

The first semester was very challenging for Janine as she tried to adapt to a new lifestyle. All of a sudden, she did not have her parents to monitor her every move and she enjoyed the independence. Despite the challenges, the first year at P & P went well for Janine, as she received all "A" grades in her courses. While Janine enjoyed her independence, she had a desire to return home to enjoy the fellowship of family and friends. Janine had been given a car prior to her going to college. It was pre-owned and had been driven over seventy thousand miles. Nonetheless, the car seemed to be in good shape so she had transportation to and from college back to her hometown. The drive however, was quite long, taking over four hours for a one-way trip to her parent's house in Petersburg.

Janine was dedicated enough to make the trip most weekends, but her parents grew very troubled about her taking such a long trip in an aging vehicle. The second year of Janine's stay in college was very challenging because she moved off the campus and lost contact with many of her friends she had known in her first year in college. More importantly, her car had more and more problems until she finally gave the vehicle up and began to stay at the college on the weekends. This turned out to be a disaster as she became bored and it showed in her grades.

Janine now did not have a vehicle to get back and forth from P & P and her home in Petersburg. This prompted her father, James, to get involved. So he committed himself to make the four hour drive to the apartment near the college where Janine was living, pick her up, and bring her back home on the weekends. This was a good arrangement for Janine because she did not have to drive on the weekends but was still able to see family and friends back in her hometown because of James picking her up. The decision that James made, to pick up his daughter every weekend and drive back home, began to have an effect on his vehicle.

To deal with the extra wear and tear on his car, James would simply have his vehicle serviced more regularly and continue making his eight-hour roundtrip to pick up Janine and take her back. He would travel from Petersburg to Chester to pick her up on Friday morning, and they both would return to Petersburg, arriving home by early afternoon. Janine would spend the weekend at her parent's house and would return to her apartment near the college on Sunday in the afternoon.

One return trip from Janine's apartment proved to be life changing in terms of both father and daughter. The day began as it typically did with James making the four hour trip to pick up his daughter. The vehicle he was driving seemed to be fine, and a tune-up was performed on the vehicle the week before. When he arrived at Janine's apartment, she packed her clothes, as she did on previous occasions in the past. Upon completing the packing for her trip home with her father, they were on their way!

As they began the trip home, the car was driving fine, so there was no cause to expect problems with it. James was in an adventurous mood so he decided to take a quicker way home that was more isolated and rural. He had traveled this way before, and while there were only two driving lanes on the road for most the four-hour distance between his home in Petersburg and Chester, it had very little to offer as far as visual interests along the route. There was hardly anything to look at on either side of the road other than trees, farmland, and an occasional barn where farmers kept their harvest. Once they left Chester, there were two places along route where motorists could stop and get refueled and maybe grab a bite to eat. On one occasion when James was driving by himself on this route, he became tired and got very sleepy. This was because there was very little interesting to view along the way to keep him attentive and to keep him awake. But he would always make it to his destination, primarily because of his car radio. But even that was not always dependable because the reception in such rural areas is often very poor. The route was simply in the middle of nowhere, so to speak.

Their drive home was on a clear day, and you could see for several miles, especially after they left the rolling hills just east of Chester where Janine's college was located. As they continued to drive eastward toward Petersburg, they could see even farther because of the flat coastal landscape of Eastern Virginia. In that portion of the state vast farmland could be seen on either side of the road, a typical scene in rural regions of the state. But there was little or no shoulder on the side in which a car could go in the case of an emergency. There would be an occasional trailer carrying farm equipment that would impede them from traveling as fast as they would have liked because the road they traveled for most of the trip had only two lanes. And while the landscape was flat, there were occasional curves in the road, so it was often very difficult, if not impossible, to drive pass another slow vehicle very easily without running the risk of a head-on collision. Because it was a spring day, crop dusters, which are very small airplanes, frequently would fly over the acres of farms below to spray crops below with fertilizer and pesticides. This probably was the most interesting part of the whole trip until later when things really got interesting with the vehicle James was driving.

They continued the drive until they were about an hour from their house when James noticed something very alarming. His "check engine" light came on and now, upon entry into a small town about ten minutes from his house there was no cause for concern. At least not yet! His engine light had come on before but this time he thought that he really needed to get it checked out on the following Monday. The reason? The "check engine" light was blinking! This was a sure sign that there were car problems ahead.

James and Janine proceeded on their way home and came to an intersection of a major highway and the road where their house was on. By now they were only about two miles away from their house. As they proceeded from this point from the intersection, they turned onto the narrow road leading toward their house. At this point James noticed that the gears in the car were not changing as they once were. But he proceeded anyway hoping that the vehicle would make it to his house, which was now about a mile away. His right foot pressed the gas pedal down to almost, but not quite, to the floor of the car. So the car could not generate enough power to make it move faster, and in fact, it was beginning to slow down considerably. Again, the road home was narrow and there was no room on the side to pull over if he had to.

As James continued and the car slowing down, they were now only a half mile from home and could see the driveway, but still it was not certain that they would make it. James had no idea what he would do if the vehicle had come to a stop in the middle of the road, but he continued on anyway. He really didn't have any other options at this point. Fortunately, this was a road that had very little vehicle traffic during the early afternoon but the prospect of having to stop in the middle of the road was not a very good feeling.

As James got closer to his house, his foot had pressed on the gas pedal down to the floor as far as it could go so no more gas could be applied. The vehicle continued to slow down almost to a stop only a few feet now from home. If we can travel only a few more feet we will have made it! James said to himself. Sure enough, as James approached the driveway of his house with the car now only cruising with no power to propel it along, the car gradually decreased speed and almost came to a stop in front of his house. He only needed enough power for his car to make the left into the driveway. Fortunately, there were no cars coming in the opposite direction as he started to make the turn. So as he was turning the steering wheel, the vehicle miraculously made it into his driveway. "We've made it!" James said happily to Janine.

James was able to make the turn into his driveway because no cars were coming in the opposite direction. Otherwise, he would have had to stop the car because of oncoming traffic. If his car would have stopped, he would surely not have been able to restart it, lacking any power to propel it forward. He simply would be stranded on the road right in front of his house! James would later find out that his alternator system had completely given out! And the alternator is necessary to help the engine propel itself after fuel is supplied. So praise the Lord! He and Janine were off the road and on their property in the driveway.

But that's not the end of the story! After making it to the driveway of his house, James still had to maneuver the car somehow to the right, off of the driveway and into his normal parking spot. He needed to do this to avoid having his car left disabled in the middle of the driveway. With his disable car in the driveway, his wife would be unable to back her car out of the garage and into the street. The solution? James was able to make that right turn into his parking spot after entering his driveway with what little power was left in his car and before his vehicle became totally immobilized. So he did make the right and the car stopped, on its own and in the exact spot that he had parked on several other occasions before: in his parking space. It would go no farther. Whew! And they were safely at home.

The interesting thing about this story is that when James and Janine took off from Chester where Janine's college was located, they had no idea of their coming experiences. God was certainly with them as they successfully made it home (Deuteronomy 31:6). Think of it this way. Because of mechanical problems, the car James was driving could have come to a stop at any time during the four hour trip from Janine apartment to their house in Petersburg, but it didn't! Also, they would have faced a serious dilemma had they experienced car problems along the rural, isolated route that James decided to take. It would have been more difficult to get the service they would have needed given that there were no service stations or auto maintenance shops in the area where they traveled. So, there was perfect timing in the turn of events during their trip home that day, and as a result, God's blessing could be clearly manifested.

As believers, we don't know what is in the future for us, but we do know that God is concern for our well being. Therefore He will lead us to our destinations safely even during times when it looks like we may not make it. (Matthew 14:30,31; Luke 24:38). Our belief helps us to have the trust we need to continue in our activities, making wise choices, and knowing that God will guide us safely to where we ought to be. God certainly had His hand in guiding James and Janine where they needed to be on that day!

> *Be strong and of good courage, do not fear nor be afraid of them: for the Lord your God, He is the One who goes with you. He will not leave you nor forsake you.*
>
> —Deuteronomy 31:6

> *But when he saw that the wind was boisterous, he was afraid, and beginning to sink he cried out, saying, "Lord, save me!"* [31]*And immediately Jesus stretched out His hand and caught him, and said to him, "O you of little faith, why did you doubt?"*
>
> —Matthew 14:30–31

> *And He said to them, "Why are you troubled? And why do doubts arise in your hearts?*
>
> —Luke 24:38

THE POWER OF SILIENT PRAYER

13

College Life

No evil shall befall you, Nor shall any plague come near your dwelling; [11]For He shall give His angels charge over you. To keep you in all your ways.

—Psalm 91:10–11

Growing up in a good, stable home environment is something most kids don't fully appreciate until after high school when they leave home to pursue greener pastures, so to speak, and to fulfill their dreams! So upon graduation, Dan Clayburn entered the world of dreams, hope, and a life of grand possibilities. It would be a time when sons and daughters understand what it is like to be truly independent. Wow! What freedom many youngsters can then proclaim! But with this new freedom comes responsibility however, and in some cases there is a cost. The cost for Dan almost meant the lost of his life!

Dan grew up in Marion, North Carolina, in the foothills of the Appalachian Mountains. He was taught basic rules on how to conduct one's self when not under the guidance of authority. As children, we often accept the tutelage of our parents or guardians as a space of comfort, assurance, and stability. Such was the case with Dan as he traveled through elementary, middle, and high school as a good student, who respected his elders and did what was told of him.

Dan's life at home was nurturing and he really appreciated that part of his early family life. His parents also were especially appreciative for Dan being an obedient child, as were the other siblings. Dan did receive quite a bit materially and, along with his five other siblings, were well trained in biblical principles and how to function and be productive in society. Despite the nurturing and protectiveness he received from home, Dan looked forward to going out on his own after high school. After all, when that happens he had wanted to work, at least on a part-time basis, and get the things that he really wanted in life.

Dan had several options after high school, including trade school and the military. Fortunately for Dan, his parents had always instilled upon him the value of getting a good education. In fact, his oldest brother had a successful military career in the air force. He had taken advantage of the GI Bill and went to college cost free! Well, Dan remembered that he always wanted to follow in his brother's footsteps, as he looked up to him as a role model. So Dan really liked the idea of his brother attending college, and he noticed especially how he took advantage of a program designed to help him along with his college education. Well, Dan thought that he would shortcut the process his brother took and go directly to college from high school and therefore forgetting about the idea of possibly going into the military. After all, his father had put away some funds to finance some of the costs of attending college.

After a pondering, Dan selected Holden College in Jackson, not very far away from his hometown of Marion.

He looked forward to receiving a good college education there, remembering how much his parents wanted him to attend college. His choice of the school had much to do with its reputation as a party school, so to speak, as well as it being known to have strong academic programs to train students to succeed in their post undergraduate careers. So Dan felt very comfortable in his decision. While he knew he would miss being at home, he was eager to get on with college life.

The first week on campus was very hectic for Dan. He had to register for his courses, and there were long lines everywhere it seemed! While Holden was a small school, there was a high demand from students, especially those students from Marion and other communities in this region to get a quality education. The majority of the students came from Asheville, which was about an hour's drive away from Holden. Despite time being spent selecting courses and preparing for an assortment of assignments, Dan found the time to participate in extracurricular activities.

While his father gave Dan a car as a present for graduating from high school with honors, he was really eager to obtain things on his own like an apartment and clothes that fit in with the style of the day! Dan did just that! Dan was fortunate enough to obtain a part-time job in the college cafeteria in his first semester on campus. He lived in the dormitory and really loved campus life! With a steady income and a little assistance from his father, Dan was able to rent a nice apartment off the campus by his second year in school. But he was having lots of fun in his first year away from home! During his first month at school Dan had purchased two suits, a variety of neckties, shirts, and five pairs of dress shoes! By the way, he also bought two pairs of expensive sneakers for the purpose of playing tennis, which he did often.

While Dan looked forward to taking part in recreational activities while at Holden, most of those activities were on the campus. There were dorm parties, Friday night socials, dance parties, and of course, there were the sporting events. The football and basketball games were always exciting to attend. Usually, after each home basketball game there would be a social gathering in the student union where students would listen to music, play cards, and just hang out. And oh yea! The basketball team had just won the conference championship the year before Dan arrived on campus.

And at football games, the tailgating that occurred before the game was almost as exciting as the game itself! The aroma from grilled turkey wings, hotdogs, hamburgers, and French fries filled the air. All kinds of refreshments, including beverages like soft drinks and lemonade, were available, but there was a restriction on alcoholic beverages. And let's not forget about the band performing at halftime! They also performed as they marched from the football stadium to the band room after the game. Being a small campus, in late afternoons you could always hear the band playing and preparing for the next game on Saturday during the football season. So there was a lot of excitement with all the events happening!

While the first semester of Dan's college life was filled with activity, it was not until the second semester when Dan's life, social life in particular, began to turn around. That's when he met Joe. Dan and Joe had similar backgrounds. Both came from good families with strong Christian training. And they both were dedicated to their studies. Despite their stable backgrounds, both Dan and Joe wanted to expand their horizons to all that college life had to offer. They thought of it as an opportunity to spread their wings, so to speak, and see what the social scene was all about.

They always were together, it seemed, and they attended as many parties, sporting events, and other social gatherings they could fit into their busy schedule without compromising, of course, their grades. So yes, they were good students, academically! They received mainly A and B grades in their courses. But because of the extra curricula activities, they grew into well-rounded young men as well.

The Sycamore Inn was a popular venue for both students and faculty at Holden. The faculty usually assembled there for lunch on the weekdays. The food in the blue room, the principle eating area at the club and to the many faculty and staff members on the campus, was excellent. Students, on the other hand, attended the facility mainly on week nights and on weekends. Students enjoyed the social activity going on, including playing all sorts of games and watching movies.

It was late Friday afternoon and both Dan and Joe had finished a week filled with midterm exams, which can be a very stressful period during the semester. So Dan and Joe decided to have dinner together in the school cafeteria and started making their plans for the evening. Fridays were special on campus because on that day the cafeteria prepared home-cooked meals for the students. Most students missed the food they got at home when they were in high school. So each week they eagerly waited until Friday when they could partake in having a good meal. The food there was a reminder of the food that most students got at home.

So while the the food that was served in the cafeteria at other times during the week was okay, students eagerly anticipated Fridays when they could partake in digesting a good meal similar to what they got back home. At this time the cafeteria menu included such items as red beans and rice with turkey gravy, barbecue meatloaf, and, of course chicken prepared in a variety of ways. There were also more healthy items available such as salads and an assortment of fruit. For desert, such items as apple pie and peach cobbler topped with vanilla ice cream was a popular staple.

After dinner on this particular Friday Dan and Joe had planned to return to their dormitory rooms and change into something more comfortable. Dan especially was eager to showcase a portion of his clothes collection at the club he and Joe would later select to attend. So after all of the preparation, they were off to some place for a night of fun.

It was common for college students to consume beer and wine on weekends. It also was common for guys to carpool as they ventured off of the campus. So Dan and Joe teamed with some other friends named Eddie and Joshua. Using Dan's car, they decided to go to one of the more popular clubs that many of Holden's students attended. So while the Sycamore Club was a popular hangout for students, they decided to go to the Campus Club. While they all went in Dan's vehicle, Joshua bought the snacks, and Eddie bought alcoholic beverages. Eddie and Joshua took care of that before they all met. Eddie was the biggest drinker in the group. Dan wasn't a heavy drinker and usually would only take a sip of wine occasionally. All agreed that they would not partake of any alcoholic beverage until they had reached the party at the club. It was a fairly large venue that was known for its clean, safe, and wholesome environment for college students to relax and have some fun after a week of classes. The club closed at eleven, very early by club standards, and served only beer and wine as far as alcohol was concerned. The club's owners monitored the intake of alcoholic drinks by its patrons very carefully and made sure that there were no disturbances among the crowd. In short, it was a good venue for teenagers and young adults to visit, have a good time, and leave after having a safe and fun experience away from the campus.

As Dan and his friends approached the club they saw that there were only a few vehicles in the parking lot. "Where are the people?" Eddie asked. Dan, who had been to the club before, knew that while there were few people there at the time, most students would arrive a little later. The evening was still young. It was only about seven thirty that evening when Dan and his friends arrived at the club. At the time, they easily found a parking space, got out of the vehicle, and entered the club. Once inside, they found very few people had arrived there, as Dan had suspected. Dan and his friends, along with about ten other patrons, were the only ones present at the time.

The evening started slow, but as the evening grew later, more people began to show up. To keep the people at the club entertained, there were many games available for patrons to play to keep themselves busy until the party really got started later. So Dan and his friends took advantage of what was available, which was quite a lot, to keep them busy until more people came to the place for the fun to really start! Dan anticipated that there would be girls and lots of music and dancing before the night was over!

Things were calm as people gradually came in, making the facility fairly crowded by the nine. So by that time, the atmosphere had changed drastically from what it had been like earlier when Dan, Joe, Eddie and Joshua first arrived. With the greater number of people came much laughter and a lot of music and dancing! Hors d'oeuvres had been prepared for the patrons, which was normal for The Campus Club. There was a long line of all kinds of meats, chips, pizzas, and drink; the alcoholic drinks were being served at the bar behind the counter.

Speaking of lines, a long one started to develop as the chef called for the patrons to come and get their food. Dan, Joe, and their friends were close to the front of the food table. As they started to get their plates to serve themselves, they heard a loud noise coming from the front door area of the club. It sounded like some sort of confrontation was taking place. And it was! Dan and Joe had a perfect view of what was happening. Two men, dressed in jeans and leather jackets had entered the facility, obviously without being invited. It was clear they had evil intentions as they proceeded toward the middle of the room where Dan and Joe were, with all the others patrons that were in the food line. There seemed to be some light resistance at the door as the men proceeded toward the middle of the building. Up to that time everyone was having an enjoyable evening.

A startling thing was that the men wore hoods over their heads, so it was evident that a robbery was taking place! By that time, the men had ordered everyone to position themselves in front of them. "My goodness!" a patron shouted from near the rear of the building. Before Dan and Joe or anyone else could react, the two men started to make demands.

What happen next was truly remarkable. The fear Dan had was confirmed: that the men had weapons. Guns! Dan and Joe happened to be in front of the most dangerous situation that you could imagine! As the men started to make their demands, they pointed their guns directly at Dan and Joe, who were at the front of all the other patrons who were waiting to get their food. Once the men had pointed their guns, they told everyone to empty their pockets and put everything they had on the floor in front of them. Of course, everyone did what they were told to do. Everyone was scared stiff! The reality of the situation was made even more frightening when one of the men fired a shot up into the ceiling, as to let the crowd know that they meant business. Dan knew that they were doing this to show that they were serious about getting what they came for and to make the patrons do whatever they were told to do.

Dan remembered the many occasions when he would attend church with his parents when the minister would talk about the value of prayer. So Dan decided that this would be a perfect time to utilize what he had heard all his life at church as well as at home during periods of devotion and Bible reading. As Dan was calm and collected during the whole ordeal, he was quietly offering up prayers for his safety as well as the safety of the other patrons. Dan remembered from Bible study that God knows our thoughts, so we can offer silent prayers and He hears us and will answer (Matthew 6:6). And while the robbers seemed to have the upper hand, so to speak, with the patrons, Dan knew that God would be with him and his friends (Jeremiah 15:20,21; Psalm 91:10,11). So, at a time of apparent weakness of a believer, the Holy Spirit rose to meet the difficulty and was evident in the events that were soon to occur (Romans 8:26–27; Isaiah 54:17).

So as the situation developed, the patrons began to give in to the demands of the robbers and took everything out of their pockets and placed their possessions on the floor as they were instructed to do. The patrons continued to follow the directions of the robbers by backing up and away from the personal items that they had just placed on the floor in front of them.

At that point one robber kept his gun pointed at the patrons while his partner picked up the valuables left on the floor by the patrons. The robber doing the retrieving of valuables on the floor got as much as he could in one large bag and then gave that bag filled with loot to the one pointing the gun. With another bag the second robber proceeded to get more valuables. At this point the robber holding the gun wanted to leave, afraid that the police would come before they left. In the meantime, his partner seemed to be preoccupied with getting more of the items that were scattered on the floor.

Surely, one would think that by this time the police would have been called probably by someone not inside the club but certainly by someone outside the club who suspected a robbery was occurring. Nonetheless, with all of the commotion, not to mention the gunshot, many of the patrons thought that the police surely was on their way to the club. Sensing this possibility, the robber with the gun shouted at his partner, "Let's go man, we need to get out of here!" Without thinking at that point the robber, shouting at his partner because he figured he didn't hear him, did the unthinkable. He took off his mask so that his partner could be heard. "Come on. I said let's go. The cops are going to be here soon and if we don't leave now we'll be caught! He no doubt did not realize that in his attempt to make his voice carry so that his partner would hear him because of the sense the urgency of the situation, he revealed his identity to Dan and the other patrons! What? Dan thought! He removed his mask? Dan asked himself in a bewildered manner. What a nutcase, he continued to think to himself, but still acknowledging the seriousness of the situation. The robber's action of removing his mask would prove to be a big mistake on his part later the next morning.

The robber that was getting the valuables finally heard his partner, and they both left the building through the front door and got into their getaway vehicle waiting for them outside. "Thank you Jesus!"shouted one patron! It was a woman who was standing near the back door, which had been locked from within during the whole episode. Finally, the ordeal that the people experienced at the club seemed to be over!

After the incident, the party did continue for a few minutes, but the focus of the patrons was to gather together and figure out how they should proceed to respond to the situation. So much of the excitement of the night had been "robbed" from the patrons who expected to have a good evening of fun. The police arrived at the club not too long after the robbery and investigated the crime scene. A few of the patrons ended up going to the police station for more questioning and to figure out ways of retrieving the items that were taken.

The robbers had apparently gotten away with lots of loot, as they used to say in the old TV westerns of the 50s and 60s. What was even more remarkable was that as the robbers sped away they apparently panicked and was going at a high speed in order to get away from the crime scene. Well, a police car was parked on the side of the road a few traffic lights from the club. The robbers tried to beat a yellow light but ended up running through a red light. Of course, the police officer saw this and turned on his siren and gave the robbers a brief chase. When the police finally caught up with them, they received a citation for running a red light. And they were requested to come to the police station, a standard procedure.

By the time the robbers were taken to the police station, Dan and Joe and some of the other patrons at the club had already come to the station to tell police what happened and to attempt to recover some of their valuables the robbers had taken. Dan and his friends knew that this would be a long process, but they did not know that the robbers had been caught! Dan was very surprised to see the robbers at the station as they were brought in because he was sure they had gotten a long distance from the club by this time. It was nearly three the next morning!

One of the purposes of Dan and Joe being at the police station, in addition to retrieving some of their valuables, was to give the police as much detail about the robbery as possible so that the robbers could be eventually caught. But again, to Dan's surprise, the robbers were there at the police station as a result of a citation for running a red light. Of course, with one of the robbers revealing his identity Dan, Joe, and the other patrons confirmed that these were the men that committed the robbery at the club. So in addition to receiving a traffic violation the two robbers, including the driver of the getaway car, were booked on first degree robbery!

Being from religious families Dan and Joe certainly knew the value of what had just transpired. They both had a spirit of sound mind where they remained calm in the midst of trouble (2 Timothy 1:7). In their own way, they too were thankful for their deliverance in such a dangerous situation.

A few observations can be made about this story. It was interesting that shortly after the robbers had left the club, they were caught by local law enforcement not for the crime they had committed earlier the previous evening at the club, but for a traffic violation. They later were summoned to the police station and were identified by some of the patrons at the club that night. The intelligence level of the robbers could definitely be questioned, given some of their actions in an attempt to rob patrons at the club.

If you think about it, some of the things that we all do sometimes if not in line with what God intends for us to do with His guidance show a lack of intelligence on our part. The difference is that the consequences of our missteps are not always as immediate as was the case for the the robbers in this story.

As for Dan, it was an opportunity to use a real, life threatening situation to draw him closer to God. His world of dreams, hope, and a life of grand possibilities were still intact! Fortunately! The event that Dan and his friends experienced helped him to be more focused in his effort of attaining those dreams in service to God and to the people around him (1 Peter 4:12,13).

> *"But you, when you pray, go into your room, and when you have shut your door, pray to your Father who is in the secret place; and your Father who sees in secret will reward you openly."*
>
> —Matthew 6:6

"And they will fight against you, But they shall not prevail against you; For I am with you to save you And deliver you," says the Lord. [21] "I will deliver you from the hand of the wicked, And I will redeem you from the grip of the terrible."

—Jeremiah 15:20–21

No evil shall befall you, Nor shall any plague come near your dwelling; [11] For He shall give His angels charge over you. To keep you in all your ways.

—Psalm 91:10–11

Likewise the Spirit also helps in our weaknesses. For we do not know what we should pray for as we ought, but the Spirit Himself makes intercession for us with groanings which cannot be uttered. [27] Now He who searches the hearts knows what the mind of the Spirit is, because He makes intercession for the saints according to the will of God.

—Romans 8:26–27

"No weapon formed against you shall prosper, And every tongue which rises against you in judgement You shall condemn. This is the heritage of the servants of the Lord, and their righteousness is from Me," Says the Lord.

—Isaiah 54:17

For God has not given us a spirit of fear, but of power and of love and of a sound mind.

—2 Timothy 1:7

Beloved, do not think it strange concerning the fiery trial which is to try you, as though some strange thing happened to you; [13]but rejoice, to the extent that you partake of Christ's sufferings, that when His glory is revealed, you may also be glad with exceeding joy.

—1 Peter 4:12–13

STOPPED! IN THE NICK OF TIME

14

The Train

For He shall give His Angels charge over you.
To keep in all your ways.

—Psalm 91:11

James had been in town at his brother's house as a reprieve from his class reunion festivities, which were about an hour's drive away in the city of Wilson, North Carolina. Junior, the lead character in this story, had lived in Ghana for over three years and had grown to love the slow lifestyle of this small community just outside of the capital city of Raleigh in the middle Piedmont region of the state. James had been with Junior for two days now and had enjoyed the time spent with him, his wife Vonn, and daughters, Jamila and Janine. They all had enjoyed a nice dinner the evening before at a local restaurant and Jamila and Janine were looking forward to seeing their uncle James again at dinner together with their father Junior. James would head back to Wilson on the next day to complete the activities associated with his class reunion, which were scheduled to take place over the weekend. Unfortunately, Vonn would not be able to attend the dinner that evening because of a prior work commitment.

So James looked forward to spending the last day of his time with his brother before meeting with Jamila and Janine later for dinner. James had wondered what Junior's work was like since he saw his brother active in finding time to tutor young people at his school, which was Millbrook High in Ghana. Junior received his advanced graduate degree in science and taught in the science and mathematics department at the school. Junior was unique among high school science teachers at Millbrook. Prior to his retirement, he had worked with two college professors from Elizabethtown University, a small college in the eastern portion of the state. They had planned a meeting to discuss activities involving critical thinking, a concept that promotes strategies believed to help students in learning and comprehending subjects such as in science and mathematics. Junior's two mentors from this college, Professors Ali and Dem, were to meet with him to discuss funds recently awarded from the federal government that would be used to train students at Millbrook for the coming school year. The meeting was to be held at a local hotel in Raleigh.

After going with Junior to listen to what he and his two college professor mentors had to say about a grant they were to work on during the upcoming academic year, they all went to lunch and talked further. Eventually, after lunch, the mentors left and went their separate ways, and then Junior and James decided to do some errands together. One thing they wanted to do was to take a trip to a local health food store to purchase some carrot juice which Junior loved. It was very good, and Junior said that it was so refreshing and it gave him a lot of energy. He had been introduced to the drink in Florida by James on a visit to his house years ago. Through the years Junior learned a lot from James about health and natural foods. He learned for example that by drinking lots of water as well as natural juices each day, the body system will be kept lubricated and, as a result, will reduce the occurrence of simple maladies like the common cold and energy deficiency. Junior found that his brother also was a connoisseur of steamed salmon, which he talks about a lot.

After a brief stay at the health food store, off they went to a local shopping mall. There James wanted to purchase some slacks for the upcoming weekend festivities at his class reunion. After going over measurements and cost of the merchandize and the eventual purchase, Junior and James were off again, this time toward Junior's house. There they had planned to relax before going out to dinner with Jamila and Janine later. It was only about a thirty-minute drive from the shopping mall to Junior's house, and it was very busy for them up to that point, and they were near the end of a hectic day.

The drive to Junior's house in Ghana from Raleigh is normally an uneventful trip, especially if taken during non rush hour periods of the day. He makes the trip at least two or three times a week; usually he tries to avoid the rush hours. But by the time Junior and James had finished their shopping at the mall, it was about four thirty in the afternoon, and the rush hour by that time was well under way. So instead of taking the ordinary route home using the Interstate highway, which is normally the quickest route, Junior decided to take the route that was less congested and therefore would put them at the house much earlier than if they were to have taken the Interstate highway at that time.

James had driven from Florida to North Carolina at the beginning of the week, a grueling fifteen hour drive. He made the trip much easier by spitting it up. He did this by having an overnight stay at a motel along the Interstate about midway into his trip. Being fatigued from the long drive once he arrived at his destination in Wilson, James rested a little, then would visit his brother Junior for the next two days in Raleigh, about an hours' drive from Wilson. He was more than willing to let his brother do all the driving while in the Raleigh area. Besides, he considers Junior a very good driver.

James would need all the confidence in Junior's driving that he could muster as they began to get nearer to Junior's house. About one mile prior to coming to White Pine Shopping Center, a large shopping area about three miles from Junior's house, he came to a traffic signal where he had the option of continuing straight ahead and going toward the shopping center or making a right turn and go down a street that has lighter traffic on the way to his house. Junior takes this route often coming from Raleigh, and he usually makes the right turn at this traffic signal to go down this less traveled road away from the shopping area. While this route is a slightly longer distance to his house than the one going by the shopping center it has the added benefit of going beneath a railroad overpass where the track runs through downtown Ghana. By taking this route vehicles simply avoid any trains that might pass because the street goes under the elevated railroad tracks.

But on this particular day, Junior decided to continue straight ahead and go the shorter distance home although the traffic was heavier going this way. Not only that, but the road would cross railroad tracks where trains would occasionally pass. When this happens, there are vehicles behind the crossing that must wait for the train to pass. It can be very frustrating and inconvenient to motorists because it can be a long wait. But this rarely happens in Junior's estimation. So he decided to take that shorter, although slightly more congested route where there is a railroad crossing.

The crossing arms are supposed to be lowered to prevent vehicles from crossing the tracks and possibly being struck by a moving train. But there were reports of problems people had in the past at this railroad crossing. One concern was the ineffective system warning motorists of an approaching train. There was a time when Junior was told that a lady with her children had approached the same crossing when a train came rushing by without the crossing arm being lowered. She avoided an accident when she was able to stop just short of the moving train.

Despite these concerns Junior thought that there was high probability that a train would not come by and that he would be able to make the crossing a nonissue. Junior's assessment of the probability that a train was not soon to pass by that crossing would prove to be inaccurate. His decision to move straight ahead at that traffic signal and eventually crossing over the railroad tracks would end up being life threatening!

While moving straight ahead passed the traffic signal toward the railroad crossing Junior seemed confident they would not be delayed by a passing train. After all, while waiting at that traffic signal he could see the railroad crossing in the distance, and cars were crossing the tracks with no signs of an approaching train. So as they came to a first curve in the road going toward the railroad crossing there still was no sign of a train. Then they came to a second curve which was only a short distance from the railroad crossing and still no sign of a train at that point. So as they approached and made the second curve, they were ready to cross the tracks which were only about thirty feet ahead of them.

Just prior to approaching this particular railroad crossing, motorists have a clear vision of the railroad to the right for miles in that direction. However, if motorists look to the left they can see only a few feet of the railroad track because it curves dramatically behind some trees and tall brush that had grown immediately to the left of the road facing the tracks. If a motorist is crossing the railroad going in that direction, it is impossible for them to see an oncoming train because of the trees and tall brush to the left.

Despite the visual obstruction that the trees and tall brush created at that location along the road,motorists assume the signaling mechanism will warn them in sufficient time. The warning mechanism, including a ringing bell and the lowering of crossing arms, should work in the event of an oncoming train. Nonetheless Junior played it safe by glancing to his left just prior to crossing the track. At that point Junior slowed down dramatically. Then suddenly, with his view to the left being obstructed by trees and tall brush preventing him from seeing down the track in that direction he heard a train coming! "Oh my!" Junior murmured. Within a second or two after hearing the train, Junior was able to stop the vehicle but only a few inches from the track! At this time he also noticed that the crossing arm on the opposite side of the track in front of him was being lowered. With the front bumper of the car being to be only about five or six inches from the area where the edge of the train would pass, Junior saw the need to back up a little. So Junior began to back up a little, and his front bumper was now probably about a foot from the edge of where the train would pass!

So as Junior backed up his car a little, he heard a slight knock sound. He then looked behind him and to his surprise, he saw that the crossing arm had been lowered! His back bumper had touched the crossing arm behind him. "Oh my!" Again Junior said with a louder voice. He could not go back any farther. He saw several vehicles backed up immediately behind the crossing arm. Of course, to the front of him now was a freight train and since he was able to move his car back a little, the front bumper of the car was only about a foot away from the edge of the passing train, a train that was moving at a fair speed. The amazing thing is that the amount of time from when Junior first heard the train until the time when train initially passed was probably less than ten seconds. So a lot was going on mentally and physically, within both Junior and James, during that short period of time that proved to be vital to the safety of both of them.

So Junior and James found themselves stuck there, pinned in between a moving freight train in front of them which was only about a foot from the front bumper and a lowered crossing arm behind them, which was touching the back bumper! What a predicament to be in! So Junior and James sat trapped in their car and endured about two minutes of the train's passing them in that position! It was that long of a wait, because it happened to be a freight train. Very stressful to say the least! But they remained calm and silent with a lot of praying going on inside both of them.

The two minutes that passed with Junior's car not moving, or,more accurately, not being able to move, was actually a good thing with the moving train in front of him. They needed to be in an immobile state to assure that the car would not drift into a moving train. So the whole situation was very unnerving! Many thoughts crossed his mind while he was just sitting there, seemingly suspended in time, not really knowing what would happen next. Before applying the parking mechanism, all Junior thought about was that he had to keep his right foot on the brake pedal for what seemed to be well over five minutes but in real time for only about two minutes. But two minutes thinking about the prospect of a moving train bearing down on you, or, more accurately, your car drifting into the moving train perhaps because of a mechanical malfunction of the vehicle?

So Junior played the what if game in his mind. Only this event was not a game at all. There was a real possibility of the demise of both him and his brother. Right there on the spot! He thought, for example, what if his right foot accidently slipped off the brake pedal before he applied the parking mechanism, perhaps because of nervousness, a seizure, or some other health difficulty? And what about the possibility of accidently pushing the accelerator instead of the brake pedal because of all the tension and stress involved in the situation? Not good thoughts! Once Junior applied the parking mechanism of his vehicle, he simply had to trust that the parking brakes and would not malfunction in some way.

Now in normal circumstances when the parking brake is engaged, the vehicle would not move. But he had only recently purchased the car, and had not yet had the chance to place the car in automatic park mode, which required only the push of a button on the front dashboard of the vehicle. He certainly did not want to experiment with that mechanism at this time. So, to make sure the car would not move Junior did engage the automatic park mechanism, but also kept his right foot on the brake pedal, assuring that the vehicle would not inch forward. So with that action the car did not move, and soon, the train would pass and both Junior and James could finally relax!

During the approximate two minutes as the train was passing, James did not say a word during the whole ordeal, and would later admit that he was traumatized by the situation. His constant thought was what if the train had derailed with both of them unable to move the car in that position? Although it was an unlikely scenario, it was definitely a possibility, albeit a remote possibility. They would have been a goner, so to speak, zapped, dead right there on the spot, James thought. They were that close to a moving train in a vehicle that they had to trust would not move, at least not move forward, into the train! And also, James, for the first time in his life, was not in control! He knew that Junior's actions in that situation would not only affect his brother, but would also affect his survival. He could only pray to God for Him to help his brother keep his composure in such a dangerous circumstance. Both Junior and James were so glad when the train had passed, and they had a story to tell about how God, once again, intervened in what could have been a very tragic situation!

Once the train had passed, the crossing arm behind them was raised and when it did, it scrapped the rear bumper of Junior's car. He did not know the extent of the damage at that point because he did not get out of the car to check his rear bumper at that time. There was a long line of vehicles behind him that were anxious to continue moving across the tracks after a lengthy delay because of the passing train, and Junior did not want to contribute to what had already been an inconvenient time for the motorists behind him. So Junior proceeded to drive across the tracks and approached the traffic signal in front of the shopping center. After the train event that had just happened, Junior wondered whether he would ever get to this point on the road on his way home with his brother James! At that point, he was just thankful to be alive.

Anyway, he stopped at the traffic signal and stayed there a while because the light was red. In the meantime, another vehicle that was behind Junior's car pulled up beside him at the traffic light. Junior realized that the motorist was behind him during the incident and probably saw everything that happened. So Junior lowered his window and spoke to a lady that was driving with a loud voice. He wanted to be sure she heard him over all the traffic that was at that intersection. First, he wanted to confirm that she saw what happened as his car was trapped between the moving train and the lowered crossing arm. The lady said that she had a good view and saw everything. After learning that, Junior took the next step and asked her if she could serve as a witness to the incident if she receive a call from the insurance company, and she said that she would. So Junior proceeded to ask the lady for her name and phone number, and she supplied both. Fortunately the traffic signal stayed red until Junior got all the information he needed from the lady. He would later contact his insurance company and supply them with the information they needed, including that one witness who viewed the incident from behind his car at the crossing. Of course, his brother James experienced everything as a passenger.

As the light changed to green, Junior proceeded to past the shopping area and was well on the way to his house, which took about ten more minutes. When they arrived Junior got out of his car and surveyed the damage. After close inspection he learned that there were some small scratches on the back bumper, no doubt as a result of the rising crossing arm at the incident site. He immediately called his insurance company to report the damages.

Later that evening Junior and James met Jamila and Janine at the restaurant as they had arranged to do. They sat down to a good meal, and finally Junior and James had an opportunity to recall what had happened to them involving the train. As Junior told it, it was a long and interesting story that Jamila and Janine found intriguing. Jamila responded that it was a clear act of God the way events transpired as Junior told it. And Janine noted that angels were clearly with Junior and James at that time (Psalm 91:11).

This story highlights the need to always be in a position to listen to and obey the Holy Spirit that is within us, realizing that He is there to protect us (Proverbs 1:33; Proverbs 2:6,7,8). Imagine however, if at the time of Junior's approach to the railroad crossing, with the train soon to pass, he was distracted by music or conversation, or impaired by alcohol. Would he have been able to stop his car in time to avoid the train? We can't avoid all the distractions that confront us every day. But it is important to recognize the fact that the Holy Spirit is always with us. But that Spirit's expression within us usually is with a gentle voice, therefore, He is only effective for us if we are not distracted, and are able to give attention to that voice. It is only then when we are ready to utilize the Spirit's urging in a time of need (1 Thessalonians 5:19; Proverbs 14:23).

After Junior had told Jamila and Janine about the train incident as they were eating, James led everyone in prayer, thanking God for what He had done for them in the situation involving the train. Afterward he also led in song as they all sang the old gospel hymn, "Amazing Grace."

The day was truly amazing! All thanks and glory be to God!

As Junior was telling the story an older gentleman was sitting at a table nearby and was listening to the whole account. After the song was sung, they all assumed that the discussion of the incident had finally come to an end. And what an incident it was! The gentleman sitting nearby then got up and admitted that he had heard everything, and that we all would be praising God in His kingdom one day, he then shook James' hand and proceeded out of the restaurant. He certainly sounded like a minister, but who knows?

Junior, James, Jamila, and Janine also were soon to leave the restaurant because all of the other patrons had left the dining area, and they were the last to leave.

James returned to his class reunion festivities in Wilson the next day, and what a story he had for his classmates! All thanks be to God!

To indicate the magnitude of the train incident involving Junior and his brother James, about a month later, Junior saw a news report that an accident between a car and a freight train had occurred at a railroad crossing in another part of the city. This time, the ending was not as good. In an incident that was very similar to the one that happened to them, two people were killed when they were trying to make a right turn onto another road, and their car attempted to cross the tracks when the crossing arms came down. Their car became stuck on the tracks when the train had slammed into it and was dragged for more than a half mile down the tracks. This highlights the blessing of surviving the train incident as Junior and James did a month earlier!

An interesting sidelight to this story involving Junior and the train is that on the next weekend there was a tremendous rainstorm on both Saturday and Sunday. As he was rising out of bed and contemplating attending church service as he and his wife did on a regular basis, a spirit came over him suggesting that they stay in the bed on this particular day. He sensed that it would be a better option than getting dressed, getting wet, and attending a church service that so many others would likely decide not to attend because of the weather. But Junior raised from the bed and repeated to himself, including that spirit which he sensed, the questions: "Stay in bed? Not to get wet?" But he responded to the idea saying, "Are you kidding me? I am alive because of the grace of God, and He should be worshipped on this day!" So realizing that what he sensed was not a godly spirit (1 John 4:1), Junior overcame that suggestion and went to church anyway, and the church was filled with believers worshiping and praising God! Afterward Junior and Vonn returned home for an afternoon of leisure. All thanks be to God, for He is worthy to be praised!

> *For He shall give His Angels charge over you. To keep in all your ways.*
>
> —Psalm 91:11

> *But whosoever listens to me will dwell safely, and will be secure, without fear of evil.*
>
> —Proverbs 1:33

For the Lord gives wisdom; from His mouth come knowledge and understanding; [7]He stores up sound wisdom for the upright; He is a shield to those that walk uprightly; [8]He guards the paths of justice, And preserves the way of His saints.

—Proverbs 2:6–8

Do not quench the Spirit.

—1 Thessalonians 5:19

In all labor there is profit, but idle chatter leads only to poverty.

—Proverbs 14:23

Beloved, do not believe every spirit, but test the spirits, whether they are of God; because many false prophets have gone out into the world.

—1 John 4:1

AN ON TIME GOD!

15

Blowout!

But without faith it is impossible to please Him,
for he who comes to God must believe that He is,
and that He is a rewarder of those
who diligently seek Him.

—Hebrews 11:6

Most of God's blessings, favor, and intervention into our affairs occur during normal, day-to-day activities that people have in their lives. No drama involved. Sometimes in the mist of bad circumstances, we are often rescued from our problems. Such was the case with Linda as she drove home from work one day.

Linda is single and lives in a condo just south of Hampton, California, which is a suburb in the Los Angeles metropolitan area. Daily routines in this major urban environment mean dealing with vehicular traffic and loud noise on a nearly constant basis and coming into contact with all different kinds of people, from the unemployed individuals who live on the streets to business professionals who move to and from meetings to lunch and back to the office where they work. There are many ethnic groups that populate the Los Angeles area, which includes a large Asian community, but all kinds of people can be found in this metropolis, and most carry on their daily activity and are fine law-abiding citizens.

In geography, there is a concept known as activity space that means that everyone has a certain area that they travel in on a day-to-day basis. Each person is very familiar with this area and very seldom do they deviate by going into other areas unfamiliar to them. In a city environment, especially a huge, diverse city like Los Angeles, it can be very dangerous to venture into areas that you are not familiar with. Some parts of the city simply may be unsafe to venture into depending on your ethnicity, lifestyle, and the time of day. But this is typical of city life in America today.

Among all the city's people and activity, Linda had established her daily routine as she traveled from her condo in Hampton to her job in the Disneyland amusement park in Segunda, a small city on the Southern California coast, approximately fifteen miles from where she lived. Fortunately for Linda, there is a major highway nearby where she lives and her place of employment, so it was a straightforward process of getting to and from work every day. She only had to deal with the tons of traffic that was normally a part of the highways, roads, and streets of the city. Los Angeles has always been known for its traffic issues, and a rapid transit system that was built several years ago did little to ease the congestion. For Linda, however, she was fortunate from the standpoint that as a security officer at the park, she had to be at work by 6 a.m., a time well before the heaviest traffic occurred on the road between her house and her job at the park. She also would leave work at three in the afternoon long before the rush-hour traffic later in the day.

Linda had recently purchased a car and was really pleased with it. The car she had before was a pre-owned older model that would need repair often, so she realized that the vehicle was causing more problems that what it was worth. So she got rid of it and was fortunate enough to get a car that she really liked. It also was pre-owned but was a much newer version than her last vehicle and, most importantly, had very few travel miles on it. For over the three years since she made the purchase, it had been very dependable, unlike her previous vehicle. She only had one significant problem with the car, and that was when she had a flat tire in the parking area of her condo. At that time, she was able to call her uncle Bill to replace the blown-out tire with the spare, and she was up and running, so to speak, with regard to driving her car.

Linda has been working on her job as security officer at Disneyland for several years, so she had established a routine in which she was very comfortable with. Given the hectic nature of an urban environment, establishing a routine is important just to function effectively with all the activity going on in the city. It is important to have dependable transportation to sustain her lifestyle. One day, Linda's routine was broken, however, and all of a sudden, she had an issue to be dealt with.

It started with a regular day at work as a member of Disney's security team. She had become all too familiar with the games and all the recreational activities common to amusement parks. And Disneyland, being the first most popular large amusement park in the country, was well established and had thousands of patrons on a daily basis. So while Linda had an important position, it was also a fun position because she had the opportunity to attend most of the events the park had to offer—on her time off, of course! She would always limit her time at many of the events because of her focus on security for the park. Besides, she could always come back to attend some of the events when she was not "on the clock," so to speak. But usually, she never would want to come back to the park for her own leisure after she left work each day. She would do so, however, on occasion, with friends or with an acquaintance.

Linda looked forward to getting off from work at three in the afternoon. She would usually plan the things she intended to do prior to eventually getting home, which would happen usually at about by five. By that time, she was able to kick off her shoes, change clothes, and relax for the evening. She might grab a pizza out of the fridge and heat it up and, with her favorite drink, watch some TV prior to doing chores around the house. She would often look at the news and see the current events of the day. Usually, the news would not be good. Hampton has one of the highest crime rates in the Los Angeles metropolitan area. And on a daily basis, you hear of robberies, rapes, killings, and carjacking. Unfortunately, this has become a regular part of the urban scene in most major cities in the country and even in some smaller areas. Oh well, such is the world that we live in.

Fortunately for Linda, the neighborhood she lives in is relatively quiet, with very little activity going on, especially at that time when she arrives home each day. After a little pizza and drink and watching a little TV, Linda anticipated doing regular chores around her house before getting into an even more relaxed mode later in the evening. At that time, she planned to watch a little more TV. On some evenings, after some rest, she would usually visit her mother, spend some time, and return home for the remainder of the evening. Much of the rest of her time at home would be spent planning for her job on the next day.

One day, Linda's routine was broken as she left work and drove home. It was a typical drive home, but on this day, she decided to stop by the grocery store and get some items that she needed.

After driving the distance from her job at the amusement park to the grocery store, she was only about another mile or so from her house. At any rate, she stopped at the store, got the items she wanted, and then left the store and continued on her way home. As she neared the entrance to her condo complex, she became eager to get to her parking space, take the groceries to her condo, and then finally relax as she normally does.

After turning from the main road in front of her complex, she had driven only a few feet in when she heard a loud pop! It was something that she had never heard before. As she continued to drive, she became concerned that something was wrong with her vehicle; she felt the passenger side of her care become lower, and the ride became very bumpy. It was obvious to her that she had just had a tire blowout! She was able to maneuver the vehicle to the side in the parking area not far from her house, out of the way of incoming and outgoing traffic to and from her complex. Linda realized that it was a busy road, and she didn't want to inconvenience other motorists using the public driving area in the parking lot. When she stopped the car, making sure it was out of the way of the coming vehicles entering the complex from the main road, she got out and inspected what had happened. She saw that most of the rear tire on the passenger side had been blown off! It was amazing that she could drive the car at all after she heard the blowout, which sounded, to her, like a pop! Obviously, the car could not be driven in that condition, with part of the rear tire having been practically blown off the rim, no doubt because of the heat that is normally generated in a defected tire and from the tire's rapid rotation. Linda found out later that the tire she was riding on was in great need of repair, or better still, she was in need of replacing the tire altogether!

Linda had counted her blessings in this situation. She thanked God that the blowout did not occur on the busy expressway somewhere in between her job at the amusement park and the grocery store she had gone to. But not only that, it would have been just as inconvenient had it blown out on a less-traveled but very busy street between the grocery store and the parking lot of her condo. What an inconvenience that would have been, not to mention the potential danger of being stranded on the side of the road, either on the expressway with a high volume of rapidly moving vehicles or on a busy city street with all kinds of activity, illegal and otherwise, going on. So she was truly blessed.

But the story doesn't end there. Linda still needed to get her car looked at and for her tire to be changed. She thought of the time when she needed her tire to be changed before when she called on her uncle Bill. At that time, he came and did what he needed to do to get Linda up and running again. Being very independent, she did not want to call her uncle to help her as before or anyone else to help her for that matter. But she knew that she really couldn't do the job herself. While she regularly does basic maintenance to her vehicle, like replacing the oil and keeping her tires properly inflated, changing a tire was a horse of a different color. She had no experience in doing that!

Just as she was standing there looking at her blown-out tire, wondering what she would do next, she saw her neighbor, Fred, drive by, apparently on his way out of the complex. He stopped and asked Linda what was the problem, and before she could answer him, he quickly realized what she needed. But she asked him if he would help her anyway, and he said he would see what he could do to get her up and running again. After about thirty minutes, Fred had changed Linda's tire. She thanked him and then continued to her condo while he left the complex probably later than he wanted to leave. For Linda, it was a clear example of how God can intervene in the life of a believer in a rather ordinary situation but in an extraordinary fashion in the way events took place to solve her problem. God was certainly with Linda that afternoon to make things right for her. After all, that is the business that He is in, making things right for us if we only believe (John 1:12).

> *But as many as received Him, to them He gave the right to become children of God, to those who believe in His name.*
>
> —John 1:12

16

Conclusion

The stories in this book, *Life in the Spirit*, represent two extremes in the experiences people have had in their everyday life. One extreme is that the lead characters in some of the stories experienced a bad situation where they needed help to resolve a problem. The other extreme is that there were times when the lead characters may not have experienced a bad situation, as described in the story, but nonetheless felt that God was leading them in a particular direction because of a unique circumstance. In reality, most of us, as believers, fall somewhere in between these two extremes.

Life in the Spirit is being aware that God always wants what is best for us. He is available to help when a need arises, but we need to recognize or believe that His help is available to us. *Life in the Spirit* means that people continue to work and function in their everyday life, but the Spirit part of us rises to a higher level when we have a need or desire for God's help (2 Corinthians 12:9,10).

In *Life in the Spirit*, it was important to portray the lead character's daily life situation as much as possible. That is why much time was given in each story to a review of some of the normal everyday activities that the characters were engaged in. The cultural environment was evident in "Double Trouble," as the lead character found himself stuck in the hustle and bustle of an urban scene at rush hour on a Denver street. Sometimes the lead character in a story is an important component of that environment, like Rose was in the "The Garden." In this case, the natural setting was described in a fair amount of detail. Rose certainly appreciated her local surroundings as she viewed from her kitchen window. More importantly, she was intimately involved with her immediate physical environment by finding a great deal of comfort in working in her garden.

Rose also had a spiritual ear, so to speak. That is, while she lived and walked in the physical, secular world, she also was attuned to the Spirit that was inside her. Her awareness of her spiritual side led her to respond to the snake event that she witnessed as she was looking outside her kitchen window. Rose was not so consumed with her hobby to the point where she was not receptive to changes in her behavior if she thought she needed to make those changes. Rose recognized the significance of the event and made a decision to adhere to what she believed the Holy Spirit was telling her: to decrease or eliminate her time spent working in the garden.

We too, must be open to change, and make decisions based on what we believe the Spirit is leading us to do. The time may come when God may guide us in a different direction than the one we may be on. God has our back. He is available to help us when a need arises, to help us transition through any change that may take place in our life.

The spiritual ear that Rose had manifests itself in people's everyday life. Did you ever have a sense to go this place or that place or to befriend someone or to make a certain investment or to go college or to get a certain job or to make some other important decision? Junior had to make that choice when he sensed a loud voice saying that he should not attend church on a day when it was raining and when the weather was just too inclement to venture outside. But a gentle voice within encouraged him to attend church service as he and his wife would ordinarily do. He quickly determined that the loud voice he sensed was not a godly spirit, so he ignored the suggestion. Because Junior and his brother were kept safe from hurt or harm during the train incident they experienced earlier in the week, he knew his decision should be based on what he knew was right, and that was to attend church and extend praise to God for His blessing.

So then, the Holy Spirit can help us make right choices based on God's will for our lives. But how do you know that a decision you make is the right one? The quietness of the Holy Spirit is described in the Scripture as having a gentle voice within. So it is usually wise to follow that gentle voice, for it will give us strength, and then we can make the right choices that provide positive results, but God always allows us to make that choice (1 Peter 3:3–4; Deuteronomy 30:19).

In *Life in the Spirit*, it was important to portray the lead character's natural as well as cultural environments; from the snowcapped mountains in "The Garden" to the hustle and bustle of an urban scene at rush hour on a Denver street in "Double Trouble" gives an intimate identity to the geographic area in which a story unfolds.

So while all the lead characters in the book adhere to a biblical base as a foundation in their behavior, their experience as described in each story indicates how they function in a highly secular society in a variety of environmental settings. The local area, where we function on a daily basis, is the place that most of us conduct our lives. We have chores within and around our homes, and we have errands in the neighborhood and city in which we live. Notice that all of the lead characters in *Life in the Spirit* were ordinary, average people. Whether we consider ourselves as an average person or not, all of us are important in God's sight, and as believers, we have an advantage because of our spiritual heritage (Galatians 3:13,14; Ephesians 1:11; Revelation 21:7). Most of us carry on our lives in a rather mundane fashion, dealing with everyday problems to be solved and issues to be confronted. The Holy Spirit within us can help deal with those problems and issues.

God can help us to go well beyond what many would consider an ordinary, average life and achieve roles of leadership and influence, if we so desire. For example, individuals that are more in the public eye than others, who might be considered successful, have the same challenges as the rest of us. This includes public government officials, politicians, college and public school administrators and teachers, those in the entertainment industry, sports figures, those in business, the clergy, and a host of other professions whose participants are deemed to be successful. But with greater blessings, we have a greater responsibility, and with greater responsibility comes more challenges that will confront us (Luke 12:47–48)! Living in the Spirit helps us with those challenges.

Regardless of our position in life, we need the guidance of the Holy Spirit. Meditation, prayer, and congregating with other believers can intensify our awareness of the Spirit that is within us. Bill Rawls certainly utilized the power of prayer as he dealt with a changing neighborhood. Upon consultation and prayer with his pastor, he was sustained while in a very negative situation, and God's grace gave him and his family favor. The Rawlses were restored to a situation where their new neighborhood was one that was as nurturing to wife and children as the old previous neighborhood once was. (Matthew 19:29; Job 42:10).

While God blesses us continually and sometimes provides favor in certain circumstances, He has to intervene in a more dramatic way on rare occasions in our life if we are to survive. Such was the case that occurred in Dan's situation at the Campus Club. Dan had heard of the value of prayer from his parents and from the church they attended all throughout his childhood. At that time he did not have the knowledge or the opportunity to apply spiritual truths to his life in a noticeable fashion. Well, that certainly changed when he arrived in college. Dan used the spiritual truths of prayer and self control when confronted with his situation at the Campus Club. He was able to stay calm and pray all during the time of his confrontation with the robbers. His calmness under fire, as well as that of the other patrons that were with him, may have been one of the contributing factors why the criminal act did not escalate to cause greater harm. There was a benefit to the trial that Dan and his friends went through, and that was by overcoming the situation that they were in, their faith was strengthened (James 1:2,3,4; Philippians 4:13).

Sometimes God will help us despite of our carelessness in doing the right thing. This was the case in "Cliffhanger." Johnson was driving at a ridiculously high speed in the mountains of West Virginia. Yet he and his friend were protected and were not harmed. What was interesting about this story is that Johnson wanted to prove something to his friend. Praying about the situation was far from his mind. He was more interested in fulfilling his will, his desire to speed, not God's will in the situation. Johnson ended up having a momentary lapse of judgment and did something he should not have done.

Sometimes our close acquaintances can have a tremendous effect on our behavior. One of the greatest needs that an individual has, according to the experts in interpersonal relationships, is to conform to others and be accepted by people who are close to us. (Fine and Winston, 2013). However, when a friend or anyone else encourages us to do something that conflict with our moral tempest, we should resist the temptation and receive the benefits of our endurance (James 1:12). Unfortunately, Johnson did not submit to the Holy Spirit within him. The result of this act of not acknowledging and acting on the Spirit within him almost led Johnson and his friend to serious injury and quite possibly the loss of their lives. In this instance, it was God's grace that kept them from a life-threatening consequence of their actions.

Unlike Johnson in "Cliffhanger," the blessing in "A Rainy Night in Georgia" was less dramatic. Similar to Rose in the Garden story, the blessing for Karen was simply a gentle voice that she had to respond to. She made the decision to obey that voice, whom she felt was the Holy Spirit. She was encouraged to continue to drive to her church meeting, despite the inclement weather and a louder voice inside her urging her to return home. It turned out to be a life changing decision that influenced her professional career for the better from that point forward in her life!

Demonic spirits are not a popular discussion in the secular society in which we live, but the Bible teaches about such spirits that have the purpose of keeping us from what God would have us to do and, as a result, from obtaining the best that God has for us (1 John 4:1,2,3). As believers, our job is to discern the Holy Spirit as separate from a spirit intent on leading us astray, and to act accordingly. Karen made a decision to act based on the more gentle voice she was hearing, the Holy Spirit, and made the decision to attend a church meeting and, as a result, received information that had a positive influence on her professional career. She was then able to ultimately complete her education and remain at the job she loved so well.

We always need God, but He is spirit, and in this physical world in which we live, it is sometimes difficult, if not impossible, to understand and relate to the elements of His reality. There are so many distractions in the world we live in today, from the images we see on television and at the movies to the information overload we get on the computer. Our challenge is to remain attentive to the Holy Spirit which helps us to understand what might otherwise be difficult to comprehend naturally or in the flesh (1 Corinthians 2:14; Romans 8:27). The Spirit within us can therefore help to overcome many of life's issues, which make us victorious in any problem we might have in this life, and assures us a place in the life to come (Revelation 21:7).

Being invisible to the natural eye, the Holy Spirit is often thought of in secular circles as something strange and mysterious. But as believers, we often relate to God when we are in trouble and the Holy Spirit is there to help us when we are in need of Him the most. Faith assures us that what we can't see is as real as what we can see, and even more so (2 Corinthians 4:18)!

In the story "Going Home" faith was important in helping the lead character Jean to transition from this natural life to eternal spiritual life, and to assist Al and his daughters to have the peace that surpasses all understanding under the most trying of circumstances (Philippians 4:7). Like many families experiencing the passing of a love one the Parkers' strong spiritual foundation got them through this ordeal.

"Going Home" involved several subplots in which faith was manifested. Among these included God granting Jean's long desire to have a day care business by arranging a rental house for this purpose to be located only minutes from her home. Also, the daughter's decision to leave her job allowed her to help Jean with her day care business when she could no longer physically do so. And she had her own issues, as she was unemployed and pondered the possibility of moving in with her parents. But God had other plans for her, and she did get the job she had long desired. And Al had recently retired from his job and was now at home on a constant basis and being able to help Jean as she was starting her day care business.

Trusting God certainly worked for Jim when he chose not to pursue an active role in trying to reverse a decision at his school that he deemed to be unfair. He probably could have reversed that decision, given his stature among his colleagues on the campus, but he decided not to take action in the matter and let God work things out for him. And He really did (Romans 8:28)! Jim ended up going to a better position within another unit on the campus where he was employed than the one he was forced to move from! And his salary took a big jump after the move.

Jack also had to trust God when his vehicle broke down in the middle of the Abysmal Swamp, after midnight, when his wife and daughters were in the vehicle. And for extra drama, there was a report that a criminal was on the loose in the area, having said to have robbed a convenience store! What was Jack to do? What action could he take? Not much, being in the middle of the swamp after midnight! His only option was to wait and trust God that he would be delivered from his ordeal. Guess what! That's just what happened! In a short period of time after his vehicle became disabled, someone drove by and saw Jack's van and, expecting it to be a friend because of the appearance of the vehicle, they stopped to help. But to their surprise, it was not their friend, but was Jack and his family who were stranded beside the road. Despite finding that the stranded motorist was not his friend, the person stopping to help, nonetheless was willing to assist Jack and his family! God intervened in the situation, and Jack was delivered from a potentially tragic situation.

Was Jack's Abysmal Swamp experience a coincidence? Not likely! Jack had been delivered from challenging circumstances on many occasions before, especially in road situations with a vehicle. In his estimation, what might have appeared to have happened by chance was actually God's intervention on Jack and his family's behalf.

And how about Linda's experience in "Blowout"? Again, God appeared or intervened, at precisely the right moment, and at the most convenient location to correct a negative situation. Linda's tire blowout not only happened at a convenient location after she had made the turn to enter her housing complex, but a few moments later, a neighbor whom she knew just happened to past her leaving the complex when he noticed her problem. So he stopped to help, and Linda's tire was changed, and she continued the short distance to her house. The Holy Spirit was certainly active during Linda's trip home from work that day, an ordinary routine activity that she had done on numerous occasions before.

Whether God blesses us, give us favor, or intervenes in our situation, he has perfect timing in our lives. Timing could not have been better when James brought his daughter Janine home from college one weekend. While driving for nearly four hours, James's vehicle was fine for most of the trip. But as they got closer to their house, the car James was driving began to have problems. The problem was that the alternator was beginning to shut down! And as they approached their house, the car continued to slow down until it finally came to a stop. But it came to a stop at the most convenient of places, at his house! They barely made it home! The car conveniently came to rest in front of the house in a space off of the driveway that James normally used to park his vehicles. It would go no further! What a miracle! The car they were in could have stopped functioning anywhere along a rural, isolated route James decided to take during the four hour trip. But God's favor was evident through the perfect timing of events.

Good timing could also be applied to the "Turn of Events" story when Al met Evelyn. After only two and half months since his wife's passing, Al had no desire for form another relationship, as he was continuing in the grieving process and was busy trying to restructure his life. Apparently, God had other plans! Al met Evelyn at a festival that they both had no intentions of attending. They developed their relationship and later married.

God's perfect timing also was evident in the story where John's teaching position which he had at Highland Community College was being eliminated. In a sequence of events, he ended up rejecting a similar position at another school where he did not feel comfortable in going even though his position at Highland had apparently ended. But wait! The administration at Highland apparently wanted to reconsider John's status at the school and perhaps reverse an earlier decision to release him. John is now in a great position. He is in waiting, having an opportunity to trust God, once again, and to see His power to intervene in a seemingly impossible situation! So the biblical concepts of faith and hope were applied in John's decision to remain at a place he desired to be and where the concept of trust is designed to sustain him in that place.

Perfect timing was certainly evident in Paula's nervous drive home from work one day on a near-empty tank of gas! She was able to maneuver her car to where it ended up coming to a stop in front a fuel pump at a local service station. Lucky? Not really. Without any more fuel, her car came to a stop exactly where it needed to be, and that was at a fuel pump! God provided favor so that she would not be inconvenienced by having her car stop on the road far away from the place she needed to be to refuel her car.

Life in the Spirit is an examination of how the experiences of a few individuals, as described in this book, have been affected by God's blessings, favor, and intervention into their lives. With a renewal of one's spirit, it is by the testimonies of these intrusions of God in people's lives that the presence of the Holy Spirit may be proved to others (Romans 12:2). Like these stories, everyone can point to instances in their own life when they were blessed, provided favor, and experienced God's intervention to their advantage. This awareness is the true benefit of *Life in the Spirit.*

> *And He said to me, "My grace is sufficient for you," For my strength is made perfect in weakness. Therefore most gladly would I rather boast in my infirmities, that the power of Christ may rest upon me. [10]Therefore I take pleasure in infirmities, in reproaches, in needs, in persecutions, in distresses for Christ sake. For when I am weak, then I am strong.*
>
> —2 Corinthians 12:9–10

> *Do not let your adornment be merely outward – arranging the hair, wearing gold, or putting on fine apparel—[4]rather let it be the hidden person of the heart, with the incorruptible beauty of a gentle and quiet spirit, which is very precious in the sight of God.*
>
> —1 Peter 3:3–4

> *I call heaven and earth as witnesses today against you, that I have set before you life and death, blessing and cursing; therefore choose life, that both you and your descendants may live.*
>
> —Deuteronomy 30:19

> *Christ has redeemed us from the curse of the law, having become a curse for us (for it is written, "curse is everyone that hang on a tree"), [14]that the blessing of Abraham might come upon the Gentiles in Christ Jesus, that we might receive the promise of the Spirit through faith.*
>
> —Galatians 3:13–14

In Him also we have obtained an inheritance, being predestined according to the purpose of Him who works all things according to the counsel of His will.

—Ephesians 1:11

He who overcomes shall inherit all things, and I will be his God and he shall be My son.

—Revelation 21:7

And that servant who knew his master's will, and did not prepare himself or do according to his will, shall be beaten with many strips. [48]But he who did not know, yet committed things deserving of strips, shall be beaten with few. For everyone to whom much is given, from him much shall be required; and to whom much has been committed, of him they will ask the more.

—Luke 12:47–48

And everyone who has left houses or brothers or sisters or father or mother or wife or children or lands, for My names sake, shall receive a hundred fold, and inherit eternal life.

—Matthew 19:29

And the Lord restored Job's losses when he prayed for his friends. Indeed the Lord gave Job twice as much as he had before.

—Job 42:10

My brethren, count it all joy when you fall into various trials, [3]knowing that the testing of your faith produces patience. [4]But let patience have its perfect work, that you may be perfect and complete, lacking nothing.

—James 1:2–4

I can do all things through Christ who strengthens me.

—Philippians 4:13

Fine, Mick, and Diana Winston. The Need to Please: Mindfulness Skills to Gain Freedom from People Pleasing and Approval Seeking. New Harbinger Publications, 2013

Blessed is the man that endures temptation; for when he has been approved, he will receive the crown of life which the Lord had promised to those who love Him.

—James 1:12

Beloved, do not believe every spirit, but test the spirit, whether they are of God; because many false prophets have gone out into the world. [2]By this you know the Spirit of God: Every spirit that confesses that Jesus Christ has come in the flesh is of God, [3]and every spirit that does not confess that Jesus Christ has come in the flesh is not of God. And this is the spirit of the Antichrist, which you have heard was coming, and is now already in the world.

—1 John 4:1–3

But the natural man does not receive the things of the Spirit of God, for they are foolishness to him; nor can he know them, because they are spiritually discerned.

—1 Corinthians 2:14

Now He who searches the hearts knows what the mind of the Spirit is because He makes intercession for the saints according to the will of God.

—Romans 8:27

He who overcomes shall inherit all things, and I will be his God and he shall be my son.

—Revelation 21:7

While we do not look at the things which are seen, but at the things which are not seen. For the things that are seen are temporary, but the things which are not seen are eternal.

—2 Corinthians 4:18

Be anxious for nothing, but in everything by prayer and supplication, with thanksgiving, let your requests be made known to God; [7]and the peace of God, which surpasses all understanding, will guard your hearts and mind through Christ Jesus.

—Philippians 4:6–7

And we know that all things work together for good to those who love God, to those who are the called according to His purpose.

—Romans 8:28

And do not be conformed to this world, but be transformed by the renewing of your mind, that you may prove what is that good and acceptable and perfect will of God.

—Romans 12:2

Documentation of Blessings, Favor, and Intervention

(Remembering experiences, circumstances, or events in which the Holy Spirit was active in a miraculous way)

1. Title given: ______________________________

Time or date of: ______________________________

Description of: ______________________________

____

____

____

____

2. Title given: ______________________________

Time or date of: ______________________________

Description of: ______________________________

____

____

____

____

3. Title given: ______________________________

Time or date of: ______________________________

Description of: ______________________________

____

____

____

____

4. Title given: ______________________________

Time or date of: ______________________________

Description of: ______________________________

____

____

____

____

5. Title given: ______________________________

Time or date of: ______________________________

Description of: ______________________________

____

____

____

____

6. Title given: ___________________________

Time or date of: ___________________________

Description of: ___________________________

____

____

____

____

For more information visit the following website:
WilliamPorterLife.com